Talking with the Bible

Scripture as Conversation Partner

Talking with the Bible

Scripture as Conversation Partner

Donn Morgan

Seabury Books
NEW YORK

Cover design by Laurie Klein Westhafer
Typeset by Rose Design

Library of Congress Cataloging-in-Publication Data

A catalog record of this book is available from the Library of Congress.

ISBN-13: 978-1-59627-234-7 (pbk.)
ISBN-13: 978-1-59627-235-4 (ebook)

Seabury Books
445 Fifth Avenue
New York, New York 10016

www.churchpublishing.org
An imprint of Church Publishing Incorporated

Printed in the United States of America

CONTENTS

ACKNOWLEDGMENTS vii

INTRODUCTION: Defining and Hearing
the Voices of Scripture ix

PART I. ENTERING

Initial Voices

CHAPTER 1. Talking with the Bible for the First Time:
Promises, Challenges, and Opportunities 3

CHAPTER 2. The House of Scripture:
Biblical Voices in Context 18

PART II. LISTENING AND LEARNING

Foundational Voices

CHAPTER 3. Talking with the Bible as Storyteller 30

CHAPTER 4. Talking with the Bible as Singer
and Pray-er 40

Voices of Relationship in Community

CHAPTER 5. Talking with the Bible as Lawgiver 51

CHAPTER 6. Talking with the Bible as Prophet 60

Voices of Continuity and Community Building

CHAPTER 7. Talking with the Bible as Historian 70

CHAPTER 8. Talking with the Bible as Visionary 81

Voices of Reason and Protest

CHAPTER 9. Talking with the Bible as Sage 90

CHAPTER 10. Talking with the Bible
as Lamenter and Skeptic 101

PART III. INVITING AND TEACHING

Final Voices

CHAPTER 11. The Bible as God-Talk 114

CHAPTER 12. The Bible as Faithful
Conversation Partner 123

ACKNOWLEDGMENTS

I have many teachers and educators to remember and thank for helping me write this book. Two of my early teachers, Brevard Childs of Yale University and Rolf Knierim of Claremont Graduate University, provided me with grounding in biblical criticism, on the one hand, and sensitivity to the formation that comes from serious conversation with the scriptures, on the other. James Kugel, who never lets us forget the ancients who shaped the biblical text that continues to affect us today, was also important for understanding the character of biblical conversation. Finally, the books of Michael Pollan, with their magical ability to make seemingly inanimate objects come alive, were both models and goals as I envisioned conversation with many biblical voices.

From the beginning, *Talking with the Bible* has been anchored in teaching and study in a wide variety of settings. In order to learn how the Bible talks with us, I needed to share my ideas with those who had experienced such conversation. I first set out the idea of biblical conversation with a gathering of clergy and laity in Arizona. I explored this further with four congregations in Oregon (Trinity Cathedral, St. Michael and All Angels, and Grace Episcopal Church in Portland; Christ Church in Lake Oswego) and at a diocesan convention in Spokane, Washington. Finally, I was able to teach courses on this topic at Ming Hua Theological College in Hong Kong and Church Divinity School of the Pacific in Berkeley, California. I am grateful for all the insights and learning I received in these settings. My students, who often became my teachers, knew well what it means to talk with the Bible.

I am deeply grateful for the support of the Episcopal Church through a Conant Fund grant during a sabbatical leave in 2010–2011, when much of my research and teaching took place. I am always thankful for the encouragement and patience of my colleagues and students at Church Divinity School of the Pacific as I labored on in the writing of this book, often to the detriment of other responsibilities.

This book owes a lot of its sharpness and focus to the editorial skills of Nancy Bryan of Church Publishing. Nancy's gifts as a Christian educator were especially important and valuable to me for this particular project.

Finally, as with all of my work, I need to thank my wife and fellow church educator, Alda Marsh Morgan. She not only helps me refine and clarify thoughts, she witnesses to a life filled with conversation with the Bible, a life subsequently filled with effective and life-giving ministry. So may it be for all of us.

DONN MORGAN
OCTOBER 2012

INTRODUCTION

DEFINING AND HEARING
THE VOICES OF SCRIPTURE

ISAIAH 40:1–2

Comfort, O comfort my people, says your God.

Speak tenderly to Jerusalem, and cry to her

that she has served her term, that her penalty is paid,

that she has received from the LORD's hand double for all
   her sins.

How do we "talk" with the Bible? To contemplate doing
so requires us to think of voices of scripture, voices that very
much want to talk with us, want us to hear them, want us
to be shaped and formed through the process of listening and
taking them seriously.

What's the difference between a text and a voice? The familiar text of Isaiah cited above contains the voice of a prophet.
That voice expresses its message in certain distinctive literary
ways, with particular intentions. The place where this text
resides within the scriptural canon also affects its overall message and use within the community of faith.

The Bible contains many voices, which are expressed
through many different texts. Our goal is to raise consciousness
of biblical voices so that we can recognize them and, finally,
enter more fully into conversation, learning from them.

We want to talk with the Bible. To do this we must be introduced to different and representative voices of scripture. Before we study many of the major voices of the Bible, it is helpful to remember our first encounters with biblical voices, and then to look at how the scriptural canon has structured and organized them. Like a choir, the placement of biblical voices is not random. Understanding where the voices are located in the Bible and how they contribute to the whole of scripture enhances our ability to hear and understand them, to have appropriate conversations with them.

Having a better understanding of the structure and shape of the biblical house or choir, we will be ready to hear some of its major voices. As we briefly introduce each of these voices, we will have four basic concerns and sets of questions. Using the biblical voice heard in Isaiah 40:1–2 as an example, we ask:

1. *What? Recognizing the Voice* (*Content and Form*). How will we recognize each voice when we encounter it? What literary forms and content are associated with this voice?

   We need to learn some of the basic defining characteristics (theological, social, etc.) of this voice so that when we encounter it, or a variation of it, in the future we will recognize it. Isaiah 40:1–2 is an oracle from a prophet filled with a message of comfort and promise to the people of Israel. It represents a very different message in a book which, until now, had been predominantly filled with judgment and doom. It is, therefore, very easily identified as something "new."

2. *Why? Roles and Functions* (*Intention*). What is the agenda of each voice? What does it care about? What function does it have in the Bible?

   Here we seek to identify the *purpose* of these biblical voices in the community of faith. The prophetic voice in Isaiah 40 is interested in comfort, in good news, in restoration—though not wanting to forget the legitimate price paid for disobedience and unfaithfulness. This is a voice intended to motivate and give hope.

3. *Where? The Significance of Place (Setting and Canonical View).* Where in the Bible is this voice found? How does this location in a larger canonical division of scripture affect the message and use of the biblical voice?

So, for example, stories about Moses in Exodus and about Jesus in the Gospels have special roles because of the canonical section of the Bible in which they are found, Torah and Gospels. Likewise, the prophetic voice in Isaiah 40 cannot be understood completely without a long history of other prophetic voices of judgment and destruction, of loss and grief. Only in the larger context of the canonical division of Prophets in the Hebrew Bible does this message make sense, providing a holistic view of judgment, salvation, restoration, and an open-ended future.

4. *So What? Shaping Conversation (Application of Agenda; Formation).* What does a good conversation with this biblical voice look like? What might a conversation with the Bible as prophet contain? What would we have to pay attention to in order to take this voice seriously? Do we need to have some of the same prophetic roles and messages of hope and restoration in our communities of faith?

Whatever the answers to these questions, it isn't enough to focus on parts of the Bible we like, the stories we like, the prayers we like. Rather, we must be ready to listen closely to all of the biblical voices, always being willing to share our own contemporary perspectives and reactions. In many ways these voices raise "so what" questions that point to the powerful shaping influence of scriptural conversation on the life of faith. The voice of Isaiah 40 will never let us dwell on only our failures and losses. Though there will be many times when comfort and restoration seem far removed from our present reality, this voice is always there to provide perspective and a future shaped by hope and trust.

Ultimately, as our interaction with the voice of Isaiah 40 clearly demonstrates, we must look at the Bible as a whole. What does the Bible, seen as a house or a choir filled with many different voices and functions, look like and sound like with all its God-talk? How will we have faithful and beneficial conversations with the many voices of scripture?

PART

I

Entering

1

TALKING WITH THE BIBLE FOR THE FIRST TIME: PROMISES, CHALLENGES, AND OPPORTUNITIES

CONVERSATION AND THE BIBLE

When was the first time *you* heard the Bible read aloud? When did *you* first read the Bible and ponder a particular story, character, or idea? Whether your first exposure to the Bible was oral or written, it may well have occurred in a fairly positive context and assumed that the Bible was worth listening to, worth reading and studying carefully, worth taking seriously as you contemplated your life as a member of a particular community of faith. All of this represents an important aspect of our conversation with the Bible: namely, the community of faith issuing the invitation to enter the house of scripture, filled with many different voices.[1]

Many of us who are members of Christian or Jewish faith communities have an initially positive experience with the Bible. Sometimes we hear it read or quoted in a service where it is explicitly proclaimed as a special source of revelation and direction. At other times it is commended to us to read and study

---

1. See my *Fighting with the Bible: Why Scripture Divides Us and How It Can Bring Us Together* (New York: Seabury Books, 2007).

individually, as a source of inspiration. Often biblical texts are accompanied by sermons or other oral expositions, giving us examples of applicability and value.

Once in a while, of course, our hearing or reading of the Bible's message does not result in clarity but rather in puzzlement or confusion. Even worse, sometimes we may not like what we've heard or read! And then there are those who would urge us to dismiss the Bible altogether, refusing to engage in any conversation with it.

No matter how we may have first encountered scripture, our focus in this book is about our present hearing, reading, studying, and pondering of the Bible, about our *talking with the Bible,* our conversations with the Bible. Talking with the Bible is a prerequisite for integrating the Bible into our lives.

Most of us have heard a voice of scripture. Sometimes it is a part of positive experiences associated with concepts and language like "love" or "wisdom" or "salvation," or even "judgment" or "sin" (especially if the concepts seem appropriate for those with whom we disagree). Those scriptural voices elicit different responses. We are the ones judged. We are the sinners. In all of this, we have the opportunity to engage in real conversation and dialogue with the Bible, hearing its strong and powerful messages and responding to its voices of affirmation, judgment, or challenge.

Today, some suggest that having real conversation is becoming increasingly difficult.[2] To engage in conversation is to experience significant give-and-take between conversation partners. Conversation involves speaking and listening to one another in earnest. These days, many say, we are often more involved in getting more information *about* something than learning of the character, shape, and desires of our conversation partner. Having a conversation with an inanimate object,

---

2. See, for example, Sherry Turkle, "The Flight from Conversation," *The New York Times Sunday Review,* April 21, 2012.

such as the Bible, would appear especially challenging. Rather than talk with the Bible, we sometimes mine it for historical "truth." In doing so, we can overlook other important messages of these biblical voices. This provides a good example of the difficulty inherent in listening to any communication partner seeking something more than information gathering.

To have real conversations with the Bible, we must be able to recognize the voices of scripture, to know what they sound like and what they want to tell us. For example, we may view the Bible as a choir composed of many different voices (and perhaps a few section leaders). Knowing who some of the major voices are and what their concerns are is critical to having a meaningful and fulfilling conversation with such a choir. Only then can we relate them well to contemporary issues and categories.

To talk with the Bible, then, is to treat it not as an object but as an active agent. It is to know what the Bible cares about, what questions it asks of community and family, why it looks the way it does, what issues it expects us to address in order to be taken seriously. To do all this is to listen to the Bible, to hear it, to converse with it.

To have the Bible as a conversation partner presupposes being consciously involved in:

- learning to recognize the many voices in the Bible,
- understanding what these voices care about,
- ascertaining where particular biblical voices are heard and the significance of their placement in scripture, and
- putting the agendas of the biblical voices into dialogue with contemporary faith and practice.

MICAH 6:6–8

"With what shall I come before the LORD, and bow myself before God on high?

Shall I come before him with burnt offerings, with calves a year old?

Will the LORD be pleased with thousands of rams, with ten
   thousands of rivers of oil?
Shall I give my firstborn for my transgression, the fruit of
   my body for the sin of my soul?"
He has told you, O mortal, what is good; and what does
   the LORD require of you but to do justice, and to love
   kindness, and to walk humbly with your God?

JOHN 3:16
For God so loved the world that he gave his only Son, so
that everyone who believes in him may not perish but may
have eternal life.

1 CORINTHIANS 13:1–3, 13
If I speak in the tongues of mortals and of angels, but do not
have love, I am a noisy gong or a clanging cymbal. And if
I have prophetic powers, and understand all mysteries and
all knowledge, and if I have all faith, so as to remove mountains, but do not have love, I am nothing. If I give away all
my possessions, and if I hand over my body so that I may
boast, but do not have love, I gain nothing. . . . And now
faith, hope, and love abide, these three; and the greatest of
these is love.

When I think of the biblical texts that first "spoke" to me,
Micah 6, John 3, and 1 Corinthians 13 are certainly among
them. And well they should be—for these voices of scripture
epitomize some of its greatest messages, touch seemingly universal themes.

The prophet Micah speaks of our need to be in relationship with something greater than ourselves and the
inadequacy of many sacrificial systems for appeasing and
pleasing God. Then, in a wonderfully straightforward verse,
the prophet sets out the behaviors that fulfill our own, and
God's, need for service, love, and justice. Though we may

have much work to do to determine what this will look like in our own lives, this prophetic voice invites us into a relationship of action and ministry.

John 3:16 is a summary of God's saving action and its consequences that no Christian wants to abandon. This straightforward statement about God's love and salvation can create serious difference and disagreement when some use it to evangelize, attempting to convert the "other." At the same time, this passage describes the "why" and "so what" of our common faith in a way that has spoken powerfully to Christians from biblical times to the present.

Finally, in 1 Corinthians 13, Paul lifts up love as the commitment and action that transcends all our striving, focusing us on the choices that make a difference. This biblical passage provides perspective on everything we do.

Viewed as a whole, these voices summarize much teaching found in the Bible. Because of this, they are often cited in communities where scripture has a central place talking about faith and action. It is not surprising that biblical voices such as these are used in evangelism. These scriptural voices make sense of our own experience, give us values and goals, and help us to hear what we are called to be and do.

THE CHALLENGES OF CONVERSATION

Sometimes, even if we want to talk with the Bible, having a conversation is difficult. Consider, for example, the following verse from the Psalms:

> The fear of the LORD is the beginning of wisdom;
> all those who practice it have a good understanding.
> His praise endures forever. (Ps. 111:10)

This verse may sound familiar. For some it may appear to be filled with promise and direction, providing clarity about who's really in charge and what is necessary for us to live well and successfully in the world. For others it may seem a bit confusing. What does it mean to "practice" the fear of the LORD? Or does "it," for which there seems to be some textual problems noted in many translations, refer to wisdom? And what does "his praise endures forever" contribute to an aphoristic teaching we might expect to find in biblical wisdom literature, like Proverbs?

For still others, this text is not confusing or promising, but all too clear and problematic. We don't like it! Beginning with "LORD," a common translation of God's name in the Hebrew Bible, this verse reeks with top-down hierarchical, masculine conceptions of God, as does the notion that fear ought to be the basis of obedience, appropriate behavior, and wisdom. To make such an aphorism moralistic by labeling those who do such things as "good" simply compounds the challenges of such a text.

So it seems that even a well-known text, one often lifted up as a summary of what faithful action might entail, can be problematic. Though new readers and hearers of the Bible may be surprised by the problems and challenges of such texts, seasoned students and Christian educators with more experience of the Bible are not. Consider, for example, the following statement from a parish newsletter:

> How many of us . . . have started *The Holy Bible*, and decided not to finish it, having gotten lost in the genealogies, impatient with the rhetoric, confused and dismayed by what seems to be a petulant and unpredictable God, wearied by the wars, tired of the complaining, and alarmed and repulsed by the concubine whose raped body was cut into pieces and dispersed among the tribes of Israel?
>
> We think we can read the Bible from cover to cover, beginning to end, as though it were a novel. . . .
>
> Many of us fail to wrestle with the text, to study it, ponder it. . . . We don't realize that the Bible isn't something

we can "speed read" or zip through, simply trying to follow the plot line. The text must be engaged, a piece at a time. We must dive deeply into it, and allow it to work on us, to speak to us in the context of our own lives, to live in us.[3]

This perceptive article, written by an experienced church educator, highlights the challenges created by the diversity, difference, and division found not only within the Bible, but also within our communities of faith. No wonder, then, that having the Bible as a conversation partner can raise serious problems. At the same time, there are programs designed to get us to read through the Bible quickly, sometimes within the space of a year, promising great benefits for accomplishing what appears to many a daunting and perhaps fruitless task. Sometimes we wish to study the Bible slowly and deliberately, particularly those sections that appear most pertinent to our contemporary faith community and culture. Sometimes we wish to read it quickly and intensively. In either case, serious conversation and the careful listening and openness it requires don't always come naturally.

The complexities of the Bible and our own personal and communal situations are only the tip of the iceberg. How do we have a conversation with a text, an inanimate object? If, for example, we have problems with the language, the theology, the cultural presuppositions, or the geographical references (where *is* Edom?), the inert Bible doesn't just pop up and answer these questions or concerns. So instead, it seems, we often have one-sided conversations. The Bible talks to us, but we can't hear what it says. We are sharing our concerns with the Bible, but it doesn't appear to hear or answer them.

Have you ever walked past a street preacher? I hear them, but I ignore them. They make me uncomfortable. Deep in my heart I believe that if I were to try to engage them in

---

3. Carolyn Estrada, "Reading the Bible," in *The Messenger*, July 2011, a monthly publication of the Episcopal Church of the Messiah, Santa Ana, CA, p. 3.

conversation, they would ignore me, sticking to their rigid (my presumption) party line on the Bible and its message. The Bible of that preacher really doesn't want to talk with me, it only wants to impose its one-sided message! One of the challenges before us, then, is to address head-on the problem of what it means to talk with an inanimate object, with something that seems to invite soliloquies on its part, or ours, rather than a dialogical conversation where both sides are heard and open to change and adaptation.

A problem aptly described by contemporary technological language, the "user-unfriendliness" of the Bible, compounds the challenges for us. There are many reasons why the Bible seems user-unfriendly to us. For example, we may not know or understand the geographical context for the world of ancient Israel and the early church. Or we may be unfamiliar and uncomfortable with the rhetoric and ancient literary forms used in Hebrew and Greek.

Alternatively, there are many reasons why we seem user-unfriendly to the Bible. For example, we may believe that certain biblical conceptions (a male god, a male-oriented and hierarchical social system [prophet, king, tribe, state, church]) are just plain incorrect and inappropriate for our time. The roots of this problem are often found in a conflict between cultures: between ancient descriptions of war and peace, for example, and our modern and very different understandings of the same. Most seriously of all, we may be uncomfortable with the theology of one or another biblical writer, which can lead us to question scriptural authority and its pertinence for our lives.

Finally, talking with the Bible often stems from a desire to root our knowledge of scripture and its voices in their historical contexts. Modern historical study of the Bible is very important. Sometimes, however, investigating and then describing the complexity of the Bible's compositional process tends to fragment the whole of the text. When this happens, we risk not hearing the full range of the voices passed down to us in scripture. When, for example, we search for the particular social setting for the prophet responsible for Isaiah 40–55, we are in danger of missing or underemphasizing the powerful new message the text proclaims: the announcement of a promise of salvation after the judgments of Isaiah 1–39.

Our concern in this volume is to pay attention to the text and the biblical voices as they have been given to us as a whole. The ancient commentators and collectors who chose and shaped the text are usually described as premodern in their interpretation. They have preserved, sustained, and created the voices of scripture we wish to hear and to converse with. Postmodern interpreters provide another important perspective for our work. Their attention is, like the ancient shapers of scripture, not on the historical settings of biblical authors and their intentions, but rather on the ways in which contemporary readers and listeners may appropriate the text for their own day. For both pre- and postmodern interpreters, then, the focus is on the voice in the text as we see and read and hear it. It is the message and activities of these biblical voices that we need to converse with.

INGREDIENTS FOR GOOD CONVERSATION WITH THE BIBLE

Having a conversation with the Bible presents challenges. Hearing and understanding a voice that is often confusing, filled with difficult or unfamiliar references, speaking of a God or a people or a king we don't necessarily like—none of this is easy. And, when we are honest with ourselves, we have to admit that sometimes the problem starts with us. We are, or can be, unfriendly and unreceptive to the Bible. The inanimate nature of scripture presents still more complications as we try to hear it, asking how its perspective might be open to change and adaptation.

Assuming that the Bible can and should be an invaluable partner in dialogue, let us view the problem from the Bible's perspective. How is the Bible to make sure we listen to it carefully and hear it appropriately, rather than run roughshod over its antiquated perspectives? How, indeed, does the Bible help us address all of these challenges so that genuine conversation can and will occur? Will the Bible talk with us?

To begin such a conversation requires looking at the Bible in a variety of different ways. Consider again, for example, that Bible-thumping street preacher. He or she uses words we all know, but often we either don't understand what he's talking about or we don't like his rhetoric and style, or we don't agree with his judgment and salvation scenarios. This is especially true when the preacher applies these scenarios to us, strangers just walking by, trying to mind our own business! The preacher seems to be imposing his opinions on us—and we resent it, or at least feel uncomfortable.

So how might we have a conversation with this preacher, this stranger? Note the parallels with the Bible here. What if this person represents a voice of scripture we didn't like? How might we gain the ability to listen to, even if we never agreed with, that strange voice of doom or gloom, salvation or joy? Assuming that we are more than willing to tell him our opinions and those things we care about, what might we need to know about him in order to have a productive conversation? We would surely want and need to know what he thought he was doing on this public square, how he wanted to affect us, perhaps where he came from and what some of his presuppositions were. Did he want to convert us? To make us feel bad? To get money from us? For what purpose? Is this to be a monologue and diatribe against us? Or, is there openness to conversing with a group of like-minded preachers and teachers and faithful followers? And what "God" is being followed? What is the basis of authority for this preacher's method? Is it sociological? Humanitarian? Theological? What difference might the answer to these questions make?

It is admittedly very difficult for some to think of having a conversation with a strange, even obnoxious, person preaching all sorts of difficult things. But the analogy to having a conversation with the Bible is far from inappropriate here. When we can't understand or agree with what we hear or read in the Bible, we are prone not to take the trouble to listen carefully, not to try to learn how it might be applicable to our lives and to our communities. And yet the mandate to listen to the Bible, to attempt a conversation with its voices, comes to us precisely because we are in such communities of faith. It is within that church community, with its great history and diversity, that conversation is not only mandated, but made possible.

Our overall goal in this book is to help facilitate *talking with the Bible*. If we are to be faithful to biblical tradition and the mission of communities of faith that hold scripture as a central part of their identity, then we can, will, and must do this. We need to move beyond viewing the Bible as an inanimate object we use to justify what we do, but with which we have little or no interaction or relationship. The special challenge before us is to learn how to hear the biblical voices, seeing them as active agents in our lives and communities.

What would it mean, for example, to have a conversation with Psalm 111:10? How might we treat the author of this text as a voice with whom we have an active, significant relationship and to whom we must respond? What must we know in order to have dialogue with this biblical voice? There are at least three essential ingredients to facilitate such a conversation with the Bible.[4]

---

4. These three ingredients relate to the questions of Why (Intention), Where (Setting), and So What (Application) in the Introduction.

1. *We must see and hear the biblical voice in light of its social role rather than as only an object of literary study.* So, for example, we need to understand and envision what the psalmist who wrote Psalm 111 was trying to do. We need to engage with the voice of someone who wants us to pray, who uses traditional theological and behavioral patterns from wisdom teachings to praise and worship God. What might it mean to have a conversation with someone like this?

2. *We must understand the structure of the scriptural house where the voice lives out its social role.* The Bible is a big book. It is structured in some fairly clear and careful ways. If we want to understand the role and voice of Psalm 111, we need not only to have a clear notion of what this speaker wants from us, but how the Psalms function in their biblical setting.

3. *We must determine how this ancient voice of the Bible is related to the contemporary community of faith.* The folks who remembered, recorded, and preserved this voice had some clear ideas about how it was to be heard and understood. We may or may not choose to follow their lead, but we are not free to ignore how Psalm 111 and the whole book of Psalms was intended to function in the community of faith. We cannot have a good, candid conversation with the Bible without taking this aspect of scripture seriously.

The fear of the LORD is the beginning of wisdom;
all those who practice it have a good understanding.
His praise endures forever. (Ps. 111:10)

We look again at the last verse of this psalm, focusing on the role of this biblical voice. The poet who wrote Psalm 111 wants us to hear the whole psalm and not just this last verse. We know this in part because the psalm is an alphabetic psalm, its message structured by beginning each poetic line with a letter of the Hebrew alphabet. Though this compositional strategy is lost in translation, we still do well to pay attention to the whole context of the poetic voice. The poet may be commending us to learn and remember this psalm, made easier (for Hebrew readers!) by this literary structure. Clearly this doesn't work for us today, and our part of the conversation with this biblical voice probably needs to acknowledge this.

This poetic voice speaks to us out of a particular liturgical context, inviting us into praise of God who is a lawgiver, a God who asks us to be faithful doers of the word, and who locates wisdom and good living in obedient, praiseworthy actions.

So let's imagine that we are being invited by this voice, like the Bible-thumping preacher, to give our allegiance to the One who provides direction and order for the world in which we live, a world often seeming a bit chaotic and directionless. Moreover, obedience to this One will bring us all sorts of good things—health, wealth, and status. So it seems perfectly logical that such an invitation would close with a call for us to join in praise of God.

It's pretty clear that this voice is not prophetic or preachy, someone standing in the middle of the town square inviting any and all to give allegiance and obedient action, followed by praise. Rather this voice is speaking to those in a particular context where worship and appreciation of our relationship with God is already acknowledged and accepted.

Ultimately, how we respond to this prayer and its liturgical leadership may well depend on how much we are able to embrace and trust these words of confidence. But unlike conversations we may have with other voices in the Bible, this voice is calling us to have a special response, praise, in light of what God has done and is doing. To be a part of this particular community of faith and to worship this God means we all are involved in prayer and praise.

MOVING FORWARD: HEARING THE VOICE OF SCRIPTURE

In an earlier book, *Fighting with the Bible*,[5] I described the Bible as a house filled with difference and diversity, filled with different agendas and functions. This house was also filled with dialogue, which enabled the house to become a home. In the present study we explore more fully what it means to live with, and in, such a house and home—to have conversations with its many voices, to be shaped by those conversations for faithful listening. Surely it will not mean the same thing for everyone, but from the Bible's perspective there are some ground rules. There are also some necessary conversations with basic voices, if you are a part of the community of faith.

As we begin to look again at the biblical voices in the hope of having significant conversations with them, we readily acknowledge the long history of dialogue we join. In that history we have shaped the Bible in many ways: investing it with many claims, often criticizing it, cutting it into snippets, abbreviating it, interpreting it dramatically through translation and paraphrase, exegeting and eisegeting[6] it in ways too many to count.

Most of this activity has been unidirectional: us talking to and about the Bible. In this study we want to look at the ways in which the Bible has spoken and speaks to us. We need to remember the powerful effect of conversations with texts like Micah and John and 1 Corinthians on our faith. They introduce us to the house of scripture, showing us special places where we can learn more about salvation, about faithful living in the world, about the One who brought all into being and

---

5. Morgan, *Fighting with the Bible*, 67ff.

6. Exegesis ("bringing out of") and eisegesis ("bringing into") reflect important ways to interpret biblical literature.

for whom all our service and allegiances exist. This conversation with the Bible is going on most of the time, pushing us into mission (direction), into settledness and home (order), into relationship (prayer), finally into praise.

STUDY QUESTIONS

- Who first introduced you to the Bible?
- What were your early favorite biblical texts?
- What message in the Bible first captured your attention and was important for your faith?
- When was the first time you didn't understand, or were bored by, the Bible?
- Have you ever thought you were talking to the Bible or it was talking to you?
- What roles did some of your favorite texts play in your faith development (such as, answer-giver, comforter, advocate, judge)?

THE HOUSE OF SCRIPTURE: BIBLICAL VOICES IN CONTEXT

1 CORINTHIANS 3:9
For we are God's servants, working together; you are God's field, God's building.

In our effort to learn as much as we can about conversation and dialogue with biblical voices, we need to explore the shape of scripture as it has been passed down to us. In a real sense we can't deal well with questions about the biblical voices—what they are, *why* they are saying what they say, or *how* we might respond responsibly to their calls for action—without knowing at least a little bit about their scriptural context. To think of the Bible as containing many voices is very important, especially if we are members of faith communities who claim the whole Bible is central and important.

We can use the metaphor of a house to flesh out a bit more fully the question of *where* biblical voices live and what difference that location makes in our hearing and understanding. All biblical voices live in this house of scripture. We need not try to set precise dates for the formation of the present biblical structure. Nor do we need to locate and define the possible historical settings of biblical communities of faith as they shaped scripture.[1] Rather, here we are primarily interested in describing the shape and contours of the house that contains all these biblical voices. It is this structure we have inherited and which we must take seriously if we are to talk with the Bible.

Many of the biblical voices radically disagree with one another about mission, about identity, about faithful living, and about God, among other things! And yet they have been placed together with all their difference and diversity in one book. Moreover, it is critically important to the shapers of scriptural canon that we embrace *all* of this book as authoritative, *all* of it as inspired, *all* of it as necessary for faithful living.

Contemporary Christians sometimes approach this scriptural building in ways that ignore or dismiss the order and structure of its component parts. This is a mistake. What the house looks like makes a difference. Where the biblical voices are located in this house is important for understanding their agendas and potential functions.

Formation, both personal and institutional, is one of the most critical effects of the biblical house. Thinking of the Bible as a building, we can readily see the possibilities of formation in light of the famous quote of Winston Churchill: "First we shape our buildings, and thereafter our buildings shape us."[2] The shaping that Churchill refers to occurs through virtually constant interaction between the building and its users. Today we tend to focus on one side of formation: *our* active shaping of the scriptural building. We do this shaping, for example, through the translations we produce and then authorize. We do this through the lectionaries we create and use. We do this through our preaching

---

1. For a good example of this kind of work, see James Sanders, *Torah and Canon* (Eugene, OR: Cascade Books, 2005), and also my *Between Text and Community* (Minneapolis: Fortress Press, 1990).

2. See, for example, Michael Pollan, *A Place of My Own* (New York: Penguin Books, 1997), 297.

and teaching. We do this through an explicit use of particular biblical texts to define our identity as people of faith.

THE SCRIPTURAL CANON: CONTEXT FOR BIBLICAL VOICES

In order to understand the structure of the whole biblical house, we must begin with the Hebrew Bible. Any discussion of the Hebrew Bible's scriptural structure must necessarily start with Torah. The importance and centrality of the first five books of the Hebrew Bible can hardly be overestimated. Foundational stories of the creation of the world and of the establishment of ancient Israel are in Torah. Descriptions of the relationship between God and Israel, grounded in promise, acts of salvation, and covenant, are in Torah. Many stipulations for faithful and obedient living are in Torah. Torah lifts up and answers questions of identity and mission for the people of Israel, placing them within the context of the whole created order and, finally, getting the people right up to the edge of the promised land, a place where all will, eventually, live together in harmony with one another and with God. This is the first and most central part of scripture, containing voices the whole people of God must listen to and converse with.

The second major room or section of the Hebrew Bible's canon, Prophets, relies upon Torah as a yardstick for the validity of the message of all prophets. Torah contains in Moses an all-important model for being a prophet. Sometimes the prophets proclaim something new in the life of the people, sometimes something disruptive, sometimes something troubling, sometimes something promising. But, ultimately, all of the newness, all of the judgment, all of the promises of restoration and salvation are grounded in Torah. More often than not, the prophets call the people to remember the stories and stipulations of Torah, to remember the covenantal relationship they have with God.

Yet for all the centrality of Torah in Prophets, these men and their message often created problems for themselves and for the people to whom they were sent. No one really likes change, or perhaps more accurately, never does everyone like change at the same time. When, therefore, Torah and Prophets are put side by side in the canon, some interesting things happen. The scriptural building is caught between "old" and "new." For example, some of the biblical voices set forth images of a wandering people, others a sedentary state; some speak of an immanent God very present to the people, others a very distant, transcendent God. Thanks to the scriptural juxtaposition of Torah and Prophets, the Bible is filled with tension. Diversity and difference are built into its structure and character. And the question before us, as it was before the original creators of this structure, is: "How shall we live with Torah and Prophets, with old and new, with the already and the not yet?"

One answer to this question came through the construction of another room in the biblical building, the Writings. The Writings, with all their diversity and difference, seek to provide answers to this basic question about living with Torah and Prophets. So, for example, one answer, found in Psalms and Lamentations, is that we will pray, with lament and with praise. We will also build community, as Ezra and Nehemiah do. We will have visions of better times, as Daniel does. We will tell stories of special people as role models of faith in hard times, like the authors of Ruth and Esther. We will follow the way of wisdom in practical and skillful living, as the sages of Proverbs do. In all of this, the Writings provide opportunities to live out our faith well, in conversation with both Torah and Prophets.

The writings of the New Testament represent the same kinds of experiences as the Old (story-telling, prayer, receiving visions), and in many ways are a continuation of responses to Torah and Prophets in light of the "new" God gives the people.[3] Some of the earliest collectors and structure-makers of this body of work saw important parallels with the Hebrew Bible. From a very early time, then, the Gospels were grouped together and seen as parallel to Torah, while the Epistles were seen as the Prophets. Acts, telling the story of the early church, the new Israel, has a direct parallel with the Old Testament books of Joshua, Judges, Samuel, and Kings, the Former Prophets, which told the story of the old Israel.

If the church saw parallels between Torah and Gospels, Prophets, and Acts–Epistles, where are the Writings in the New Testament? One plausible thesis is that the whole New Testament represents an extension of the Writings. Then the diversity and difference in the New Testament becomes an extension of biblical voices calling for faithful obedience to Torah and Prophets, albeit in the midst of some very new actions by God.

It makes a difference where a biblical voice is located in these larger scriptural divisions. To cite but one example, stories originally function as voices of testimony and witness. These stories are then shaped into larger literary complexes with different functions and intentions. These complexes are then collected and shaped into still larger divisions, namely Torah, Prophets, Writings, Gospels, and Epistles. The "original" intentions of the storytellers and singers and pray-ers are colored and nuanced by the functions and intentions of the larger divisions, or rooms in the biblical house, of which they are now a part.

Later communities of faith would have heard the earlier biblical voices in ways that imbue those voices with new power and authority. This again is a part of the formation process referred to by Churchill. If, for example, Torah is a particular part of the house where certain voices are heard, then the voices in it are vested with a specific authority and import because of their location. There is, then, good reason to pay attention to the shape and function of the biblical house of voices.

---

3. See, for example, Morgan, *Between Text and Community*, 76–107.

FAVORITE TEXTS IN THEIR SCRIPTURAL CONTEXT

Returning to texts we examined in chapter 1, what difference does their setting in the scriptural canon make for the way we hear their voices? Micah 6:6–8, for example, a prophetic voice, is very hard to understand unless we know something about that most important of biblical rooms: Torah. The opening questions about sacrifice are related to stories, or sacrificial schedules, in Torah. Anyone who doesn't know what Torah calls for in terms of sacrifice will have a problem understanding Micah. And when the prophet turns the tables and begins to answer the questions, saying "He has told you what is good," again the reference is to Torah. That's where we are told what is good. Interestingly, the prophet is inviting us to be a part of a scriptural conversation, for he gives several different options for faithful living in these three verses, and they all come from and are justified by Torah! The prophet's message compels us to be grounded in Torah, even as we evaluate which of its many stories will best represent God's will for us in our own particular time and place.

John 3:16 also has parallels with Torah, though not as explicitly as the prophet Micah. Instead, John's teaching assumes its centrality in part because of its concise summary of God's loving action to us and the whole world. But it is the fact that the Gospels have been lifted up and made central for the whole of the New Testament—as Torah is for the Hebrew scriptures—that makes this verse glow with authority. We have many similar teachings in the Johannine letters, for example. But these do not have the status and central visibility for the Christian community that the Gospels have. Yes, there are significant differences between this verse and the teachings of Torah. But the structure of the biblical house lends its hand in making this verse stand out authoritatively.

In 1 Corinthians 13, Paul adds an essential ingredient to the task of being a faithful follower of Jesus Christ. As with Micah, Paul is inviting a conversation with scripture, injecting an important component, love, into that which is necessary to accomplish our various ministries well. Like Micah, Paul is asking us to consider some foundational actions to accompany whatever form of ministry engages us. In doing so, he is implicitly reminding us that such motivation and action is rooted in God's own love to us and the whole world, something frequently proclaimed in both Torah and the Gospels. By appearing to state the obvious, Paul is probably criticizing a number of folks who are not acting in this way. In this critique, Paul functions as a prophet, providing a message that functions as a two-edged sword, bringing comfort and confidence to some, judgment and a call to serious reevaluation of action to others.

Finally, in Psalm 111, we encounter a person of prayer, a composer whose voice reflects wisdom and sages, steeped in Torah, sensitive to poetry and liturgy. As a part of the Writings, this psalmist's voice calls us to profess our faith, especially through praise, prayer, and community worship. The psalmist reminds us of the final purposes of Torah, Prophets, Gospels, and Epistles. This is a central part of what the Writings, at their best, do.

BUILDING THE BIBLE WITH VOICES: AN OVERVIEW

Eventually all biblical voices come together in Torah, Prophets, Writings, Gospels, Acts, and Epistles. We can think of this process as a construction project. Building the scriptural canon consists of at least three separate phases: first, the original utterances or writings; second, community collections and compositions; and finally, canonical divisions. Like physical buildings, especially those built over a long period of time, these phases can sometimes occur simultaneously.

1. *Original Utterances or Writings*. Biblical voices come from prophets, seers, apostles, cultic leaders, storytellers, poets,

and many more. These voices are expressed in individual prayers, as stories about patriarchs, as epiphanies, as letters, as records of one variety or another, as oracles, and much more (laws, letters, visions). They could be oral or written, they could be collected or not, depending on their own intrinsic merit or the importance of remembering a patriarch or a prophet.

2. *Community Collections and Compositions*. The second phase of construction involves larger communities of faith. Regardless of their origins and first intentions, all biblical voices are now a part of communal traditions and writings. Often, for example, smaller voices become a part of much larger stories. Now, for example, stories about Abram and Abraham are used to speak of the origins and purposes of Israel in a new land. Or the stories about David and Solomon, originally told to lift up important characteristics of these kings, are now a part of a much larger history of Israel and Judah in the land.

3. *Canonical Divisions*. Finally, of course, collections of biblical voices, some of them originally oral and some written, are *all* put together in the canon of scripture: into Torah or Prophets or Writings or Gospels or Acts or Epistles. Sometimes this causes the voices, again, to serve other, larger, purposes. Now, for example, the stories of Abraham are not merely there to tell us about the patriarch's faith and travels, or to help us understand how Abraham is connected to the other patriarchs, nor even about how early Israel got to Egypt. Now the voice of Abraham's storyteller is a part of a grand epic reaching from Mesopotamia to the banks of the Jordan, where Israel is poised and ready to become the people of God in a new land. And, of course, David and Solomon and, most of all, Moses are tied to much larger collections of psalms, of proverbs, of laws.

The same thing happens in the New Testament. We begin with voices telling the stories of Jesus and his healing acts, his calls to repentance, his wisdom teachings. Then these voices are made a part of larger complexes, becoming part of particular gospels with broad and inclusive claims about who Jesus was, and what difference those claims can and should make for a particular faith community and the world it lives in. Finally, in a more informal but equally effectual way, the New Testament is divided into at least two major divisions, Gospels and Epistles, intentionally parallel to Torah and Prophets.

THE BUILDING'S AFTERLIFE: SCRIPTURAL FORMATION

Finally, then, the Bible is completed. Scripture's canon is structured and its contents set. No more can be added or subtracted—at least not officially. But, talking with the Bible is just beginning, and with it the shaping and reshaping of the people of God. Remember, Churchill said the building would shape us after we built it. It has, and will continue to do so!

One of the ways in which the scriptural building shapes us is through its particular perspective on the world, a perspective we gain from being inside the house, within our particular Christian communities of faith. The structures of Torah, Prophets, and Gospels act very much like windows to the world. Windows provide a way for folks inside the building to see out. Windows also provide a "frame" to that world outside. In *A Place of My Own*, Michael Pollan speaks of the window in a building he has helped to build. It was an old-fashioned, almost anachronistic window composed of six panes of glass divided by a grid of mullions. In describing the new view and perspective provided by this window, Pollan writes: "What had been a single uninflected horizontal view out over the desk was now divided into six discrete square frames. The surprise was just how much more you could see this way, now there were six focal points instead of one, and twenty-four edges composing the scene instead of four."[4] Think of the Bible as a window, with each of its many voices, providing a frame for us to see God and people in the world. From inside or outside, this is quite a building. The view of the world is nuanced, placed into a grid that divides and unifies at the same time.

Through generations of critical scholarship, we have studiously looked at the history of biblical composition, trying to determine exactly how and when and why the Bible came to look like what it does now. In many cases we have been successful, providing a rich picture of textual development and interaction with the communities of faith that have created and been touched by biblical voices. But there is a limit to our ability to figure this out with precision. The structures of canon are clear enough. We may know some of the possible motivations or rationales for putting originally independent voices together in Torah or Gospels. Finally, however, it doesn't matter whether we know the rationale for the structure or the precise time in which a text was created or the names of its authors, collectors, and redactors. What we are left with are the voices of scripture, in a particular canonical house that provides an important context for our ability to understand the "so what" of these voices for ancient Israel, for the early church, *and* for us today. To illustrate this point and its potential power for formation, we return to Michael Pollan:

> The architect borrows from the past by adapting successful patterns, the ones that have been proven to support the kind of life the place hopes to house—porches and watching the world go by, for example. But what about the time to come? . . . It seems to me there is another, more profound way an architect can open a building to the impress of its future. Forswearing a totalitarian approach to its details, the architect can instead leave just enough play in his design for

---

4. Pollan, *A Place of My Own*, 260.

others to "finish it"—first the craftsmen, with their particular knowledge and sense of the place, and then the inhabitants, with their stuff and with the incremental changes that, over time, the distinctive grooves of their lives will wear into its surfaces and spaces. It may be that making a great place, as opposed to a mere building or work of architectural art, requires a collaboration not so much in space as over time.[5]

Is not the Bible building much like the "great place" Pollan describes? How would the ancients who shaped the scriptures want us to interpret the voices they contain?[6] Would they have the same kind of frustrations with contemporary users searching for the historical grounding of their message as some architects have with folks who live in and use their building after completion? Or not? And must not we, like the ancient composers of the scriptural canon, describe and interpret what happens in our formation when we talk with the Bible, as something God does with and for us? It is now time to identify and listen to those voices, which still shape us toward faithfulness.

STUDY QUESTIONS

- In what parts of the scriptures (Torah, Prophets, Writings, Gospels, Acts–Epistles) are your favorite biblical texts?
- What are some of the important messages you find in each of the major divisions of scripture?
- Who are some of the major people in each of these divisions?
- Do you think one of the scriptural divisions is most important or least important? Why or why not?

---

5. Pollan, *A Place of My Own*, 275.
6. See James Kugel, *How To Read the Bible: A Guide to Scripture Then and Now* (New York: Free Press, 2007), especially 5–24, for a description of some of these ancient shapers and interpreters of scripture.

PART

II

Listening and Learning

3

TALKING WITH THE BIBLE AS STORYTELLER

DEUTERONOMY 26:5–9

You shall make this response before the LORD your God: "A wandering Aramean was my ancestor; he went down into Egypt and lived there as an alien, few in number, and there he became a great nation, mighty and populous. When the Egyptians treated us harshly and afflicted us, by imposing hard labor on us, we cried to the LORD, the God of our ancestors; the LORD heard our voice and saw our affliction, our toil, and our oppression. The LORD brought us out of Egypt with a mighty hand and an outstretched arm, with a terrifying display of power, and with signs and wonders; and he brought us into this place and gave us this land, a land flowing with milk and honey."

MARK 1:14–15

Now after John was arrested, Jesus came to Galilee, proclaiming the good news of God, and saying, "The time is fulfilled, and the kingdom of God has come near; repent, and believe in the good news."

JOHN 21:25

But there are also many other things that Jesus did; if every one of them were written down, I suppose that the world itself could not contain the books that would be written.

It is hard to imagine a more important voice of scripture than that of the storyteller. Surely a good case can be made that this was the *first* voice of scripture; that telling stories about special people, about special revelations, about special places is the heart of the Bible. Some might make a case that there are more important confessional, liturgical, or legal texts, but the stories contained in the Bible represent a necessary perspective for any community of faith—providing a witness to foundational experiences and leaders, without which we could not and would not be who and what we are today.

WHAT? RECOGNIZING THE VOICE

The voice of the storyteller in the Bible is fairly easy to recognize. Unlike some other societies that use epic poetry to tell the stories of their most significant leaders, foundational events, sacred sites, and gods, the Hebrew Bible and the New Testament tend to do this in prose. Indeed, most biblical stories are relatively short, betraying, for most of them, an oral provenance. These are the kinds of stories we often hear over the dinner table or as asides in meetings and other social occasions. Did you hear what happened to Abraham today? Did you know how this place got its name and why it is so special? By the time stories like this become a part of the Bible's voice, they have almost always been combined with other stories to serve purposes much different than their original intention. So, for example, a story about Abram and Sarai (Genesis 12:10–20), which may have had the purpose of describing how beautiful Sarai was, or how cowardly Abram was, or how dastardly Pharaoh was, is now a vehicle to describe the circuitous route Abram takes to fulfill the promises God has made to him about land and progeny. It has been tied together with many other stories about Abraham and Sarah, about Isaac and Rebekah, about Jacob and his family. So it is with Jesus and the other stories told of him as healer and sage and outspoken critic, now combined in different gospels for larger purposes, often with quite different audiences.

So, we hear the voice of the Bible as storyteller with several stories brought together to form narratives that have larger purposes than the original smaller stories. We can easily recognize the smaller story units in scripture. Indeed, our contemporary lectionaries and sermons usually focus on these units rather than the larger entities of which they are a part. Because these stories were originally independent, it is often easy to see the added introductions and conclusions required to fit the story into the larger complex of which they are now a part. Many stories have an obvious "so what" ending, which stresses a particular result, or a movement from one place to another, or some other consequence. For example, after the story in Genesis relating Jacob's wrestling with God, we read: "So Jacob called the place Peniel [face of God], saying, 'For I have seen God face to face, and yet my life is preserved'" (Genesis 32:30). Here the "so what" relates to a place, answering the question of how this name came to be.

The voice of the Bible as storyteller often focuses on the personal, describing traits of heroes or villains, lifting up values like faithfulness or allegiance, honesty or dishonesty. The voice can speak candidly and clearly about the character of leaders and their families, often drawing us into the story in ways that make us care deeply. The voice of the storyteller is easy to remember. Whether complimenting and praising or castigating and judging, the voice is inherently interesting and often compelling. Examples of the storyteller voice in the Bible include cycles of stories about the patriarchs and their families, Moses and his family, the judges and their great adventures, Samuel and Saul, David and Bathsheba, David and Goliath, Solomon, Elijah and Elisha, Jesus and the disciples, Paul and Barnabas, Peter and James.

WHY? ROLES AND FUNCTIONS

Scholars often differentiate biblical stories on the basis of their perceived purpose. Sometimes this is easy to determine. There may be a blatantly obvious formula or turn of phrase to summarize the actions and significance of the story. While hinting at the story's original function, these endings are markers, helping us see transitions and, sometimes, an editorial thread that ties the stories together. For example, the short story of Rachel's death and Benjamin's birth in Genesis ends with these words: "And Jacob set up a pillar at her grave . . . which is there to this day. Israel journeyed on, and pitched his tent beyond the tower of Eder" (Genesis 35:20–21). These verses note both the establishment of a shrine and a continuation of Jacob's journey, perhaps indicating not one but two editors or collectors trying to make sense of the story and integrating it into a larger voice.

One primary intention of the storyteller voice is straightforward and transparent: to provide a vehicle for remembering. With regard to the Bible, then, it is to remember that Abraham was faithful and wise; that we are in the land of Canaan, at once a hostile and a promising place because God gave it to us; that David was human, possessing all sorts of human frailties, but was also the paradigm for king; that Jesus was a healer, called to a particular mission, who did things most of us don't and can't do. The Bible as storyteller introduces us to particular adventures, travels, dangers, obstacles faced by leaders and peoples. These people and their land become carriers of special values we are to remember and emulate. The Bible as storyteller exposes us to values, character traits, salvation events, sacred spaces, foreigners, threats to unity, God's purposes for the people, and more.

The voice of the storyteller provides us with the fabric of the Bible, that which ties all of this diverse and different literature together. It witnesses to a larger story of our relationship to one another and to God; a story that makes most sense in the context of these smaller stories about God and Jacob, God and David, God and Jesus.

The Bible as storyteller is rarely neutral. There are some explicit intentions associated with these stories. There is more often than not a moral, a particular point (or several) the story-teller wants to make. To assess this intention we need to take seriously the larger scope of the story, focusing on the bigger units to which the smaller stories now belong. So the wisdom and healing stories of Jesus must now be related to the overall intentions of the whole Gospel story, and the particular actions of Moses must be related to the larger story of Israel's exodus from Egypt and, finally, entry into the promised land.

Perhaps the best way to come to grips with the intentions of the storyteller is to try to answer two questions: "Why are we being told this story?" and "What does the storyteller want us to remember?" Answering these questions does not neces-sarily require us to know the historical setting of the authors. We must, however, make connections between biblical stories, looking at the larger framework that ties them together. We want to know, for example, why all these stories about Moses or Jesus or David or Solomon or Joseph are collected and tied together. What was the author trying to tell us?

WHERE? THE SIGNIFICANCE OF PLACE

The voice of the storyteller presupposes an audience! Stories are for groups that will use the stories in particular ways and preserve them for posterity. Sometimes these are small and discrete groups, like the families of Abraham and Isaac and Jacob. Sometimes they are tribes or clans, expanded families. Sometimes they are institutions that claim specific stories and make them their own, like the city of Jerusalem or the states of Israel and Judah. And, of course, many of these groups or institutions want to share their stories with others, sometimes for evangelistic purposes but also to justify their own "place" in society and the world.

Stories, of course, are found all over the Bible. The voice of the storyteller is prolific. The storyteller helps to shape many of the books in the Bible. For example, viewed from one perspective, Genesis traces the history of the world and the beginnings of the people of Israel from creation to Egypt. In many ways the book of Genesis is a collection of stories that takes us along that path. Yes, there are many other voices in the book of Genesis, but without the voice of the storyteller, this book would not exist in the form it does now. One can make the same type of argument for the Gospels in the New Testament. These stories in both Old and New Testaments are a primary vehicle for structuring and highlighting content critical to many books in Torah and Gospels.

There are, however, stories in all parts of the Bible. The Prophets have many stories about particular experiences of these special people. And in the Former Prophets (Joshua, Judges, Samuel, and Kings) and Acts, the histories of Israel, Judah, and the early church are filled with stories about Samuel, Saul, David, Paul, Barnabas, Peter, and so many, many more.

There are significant differences in the voices of the storyteller, depending on where that voice is heard. The stories of Jesus in the Gospels or of Jacob in Genesis present us with foundational understandings of our families, our clans or tribes, our states, our church. These stories lift up significant people, significant events (the exodus, the crucifixion and resurrection), making them normative and essential for understanding who we are and where we came from. More than this, these stories trace a history of salvation that continues to the present day, providing us with values and direction for the future, following in the steps of Jesus or Abraham or . . . ?

The storytellers we find in the Prophets and the Epistles have different purposes to accomplish. Yes, we will still have stories about major figures, like Jeremiah or Paul, but now the focus is on their message. Given the fact that prophets are messengers and that epistles (or letters) are messages as well, it makes perfect sense for the storyteller to want to enhance and solidify the message through pertinent accounts about the lives of the prophets and apostles.

The storyteller in the Writings is not interested in building foundations; that's already been done. Nor are there prophetic messengers to tell stories about, although many of the stories about Daniel, a seer and visionary, come close to serving this function (see chapter 8). Rather, through wonderful stories in books like Ruth and Esther, the storyteller focuses on recounting challenges and successes in living out faith in the world. In these books the nature of the world, with all of its threats and opportunities for faithful service, is the substance of the storyteller's message. All of this is congruent with the function of the Writings themselves, living in the tension of Torah (a given identity, the "old") and Prophets (a call to remember the past in light of "new" events that will bring forth change). Ruth and Esther, so very different in their messages, are both speaking powerfully to what it means to live faithfully in the world.

SO WHAT? SHAPING CONVERSATION

If we take seriously the voice of the Bible as storyteller, what would our conversation look like? The storyteller knows that Israel and the new Israel (the church) are special. They have experienced revelations. They have experienced defeat and death. They have experienced rebirth and new life. They know who they are and where they are going. They know some of the most important family highlights, and they remember why these stories were told and why they are important. The storyteller is clear about identity. The storyteller is motivated and excited; the storyteller is witnessing to the story of God's people in the world.

So, in the context of the world we live in today, what does conversation look like? What do we do differently because we have heard these stories in the midst of faith communities that consider them normative for faithful living? How are we shaped by these stories? What does formation mean for the person who talks with the Bible as storyteller?

First, perhaps, we will remember and retell the individual stories, understanding how they fit together and what difference they make for describing where we came from, who we are now, and where we are going. The creedal-like recitation in Deuteronomy 26 traces Israel's journey from foreign lands to the promised land, to Egypt, and to the promised land once more. We too must know this story. According to Deuteronomy, we are to recite this story before God (which means in the context of worship) and at times when we are gathered together to remember (Deuteronomy 26:5–11). The storyteller demands *we*, the people of God, do this. These stories do not belong to the individual, but to all of us who have experienced this wonderful story. In Deuteronomy, however, very much like the church in the world today, there are many who do not belong to Israel, who have not experienced the story. We are to tell the story to one another, to be sure, but whenever possible we are to share it with others as well. The act of witness is an important part of taking the Bible as storyteller seriously. The model of Jesus in the Gospels of Mark and John highlights this aspect of the storyteller and our conversation.

Another way in which talking with the Bible as storyteller can shape us involves how seriously we take the images of the biblical leaders found in story. As the columnist David Brooks wrote recently, speaking of leadership:

But the main problem (in thinking straight about authority) is our inability to think properly about how power should be used to bind and build. Legitimate power is built on a series of paradoxes: that leaders have to wield power while knowing they are corrupted by it; that great leaders are superior to their followers while also being of them; that the higher they rise, the more they feel like instruments in larger designs. . . . To have good leaders you have to have good followers—able to recognize just authority, admire it, be grateful for it and emulate it.[1]

To listen to the stories about biblical leaders is to address some of the issues Brooks has identified. The paradoxes of power and the corrupting effects of leadership are also reflected in the stories of Jacob, David, and other biblical heroes. To talk with the Bible as storyteller may demand we call into question some contemporary approaches to leadership and authority, as seen in "Question Authority" stickers and some of the rhetoric of the Occupy movements.

Finally, to take the biblical storytellers seriously pushes us to worship, which involves both praise and lament. Praise, first and foremost, is the response to all that God has done with us and for us—told so movingly in story. Lament is present because for all the wonderful acts of God, there is great disparity between what has been and what is, what is and what is meant to be—at least as these stories tell us. So now we go to another major voice of the Bible: pray-er and singer!

---

1. David Brooks, "The Follower Problem," *The New York Times*, Opinion Pages, June 11, 2012.

STUDY QUESTIONS

Pick a favorite biblical story (or maybe two, one Old Testament and one New Testament), and briefly describe this voice by providing some answers to the following questions[2]:

- *What? Recognizing the Voice (Content and Form).* What does the voice of the storyteller that you have chosen look like?
- *Why? Roles and Functions (Intention).* What is the agenda of the storyteller in this text? Why is this story written and passed down to us?
- *Where? The Significance of Place (Setting and Canonical View).* In what particular part of scripture is this story found? How does this placement add to its meaning?
- *So What? Shaping Conversation (Application of Agenda; Formation).* Think of a situation in which this particular biblical voice might be especially valuable. What does a good conversation with this voice for the situation you have chosen look like? What positive things might this voice suggest? What new things might the voice suggest? Things you weren't necessarily looking for or maybe don't even want, but this voice wants factored in. . . .

---

2. For a fuller set of questions on these subjects, see the Introduction (pp. x–xii).

4

TALKING WITH THE BIBLE AS SINGER AND PRAY-ER

EXODUS 15:21

And Miriam sang to them:

"Sing to the LORD, for he has triumphed gloriously;
horse and rider he has thrown into the sea."

PSALM 138

Of David.

I give you thanks, O LORD, with my whole heart;
    before the gods I sing your praise;
I bow down toward your holy temple
    and give thanks to your name for your steadfast love
    and your faithfulness;
for you have exalted your name and your word
    above everything.
On the day I called, you answered me,
    you increased my strength of soul.

All the kings of the earth shall praise you, O LORD,
    for they have heard the words of your mouth.
They shall sing of the ways of the LORD,
    for great is the glory of the LORD.
For though the LORD is high, he regards the lowly;
    but the haughty he perceives from far away.

Though I walk in the midst of trouble,
    you preserve me against the wrath of my enemies;
    you stretch out your hand,
    and your right hand delivers me.
The LORD will fulfill his purpose for me;
    your steadfast love, O LORD, endures forever.
    Do not forsake the work of your hands.

LUKE 1:46–55
And Mary said,
"My soul magnifies the Lord,
    and my spirit rejoices in God my Savior,
for he has looked with favor on the lowliness of his servant.
Surely, from now on all generations will call me blessed;
    for the Mighty One has done great things for me,
    and holy is his name.
His mercy is for those who fear him
    from generation to generation.
He has shown strength with his arm;
    he has scattered the proud in the thoughts of their hearts.
He has brought down the powerful from their thrones,
    and lifted up the lowly;
he has filled the hungry with good things,
    and sent the rich away empty.
He has helped his servant Israel,
    in remembrance of his mercy,
according to the promise he made to our ancestors,
    to Abraham and to his descendants forever."

WHAT? RECOGNIZING THE VOICE

Like the voice of the storyteller, the voice of the Bible as singer
and pray-er is surely one of the earliest and most important. Like
the storyteller, the singer and pray-er is a constant presence in

the Bible, reflecting actions and messages central to all times and places. Texts like the Song of Miriam or the Song of Deborah (Judges 5) or the Song of Hannah (1 Samuel 2) are all good examples of this voice.

More often than not, the voice of song or prayer is expressed in poetry. In Hebrew, this will result in many types of parallelism. Sometimes such poetry reflects an oral origin. In all cases, however, the poetic character of songs and prayers aid in their transmission in terms of both content (*this* is like, or not like, *that*) and form. Parallelism is used to emphasize, to contrast, to nuance, to list, to compare—all of which can be structured in prayers and songs to make them more easily repeated and remembered. Prayers and songs also invite others into their activity. So, whether or not Miriam or Deborah or Hannah originally uttered their songs of triumph and thanksgiving, by the time they are incorporated into the biblical canon and become a part of its voice to us they have moved from the expression of individual song and prayer to communal praise. They now belong to the whole community, and we are invited into their sphere.

The Bible boldly includes the breadth of human experience as appropriate for the voice of singer and pray-er. This voice covers the range of human emotion. There are, to be sure, favorite topics. The king and other leaders of the people such as warriors, judges, patriarchs, and cultic officials are frequent subjects. So too are the difficult but inevitable events in human life: war, illness, death, oppression, betrayal, and enemies of every stripe. Catastrophes are also common subjects, used either as threat or in prayers of deliverance. Joy, accompanied by gratitude for the gift of life, also permeates the voice of song and prayer in the Bible.

Sometimes this voice is actively involved in addressing the puzzles of life. Why bad things happen to good people or why good things happen to bad people are often topics of prayer.

Praise and thanksgiving for victory and deliverance, or petition for victory and salvation in the midst of difficult times
are also common. Sometimes this voice is a poetic equivalent
of the storyteller, listing all the reasons we should be grateful
for a particular leader's attributes in governance or military
endeavors. Finally, last but far from least, the biblical voice of
singer and pray-er can be concerned with the apparent presence, or absence, of God in the life of the individual and the
community of ancient Israel.

In attempting to recognize the forms of song and prayer
in the Bible, the most significant characteristic is the explicit
address of God. More often than not, this voice is filled with
elements of praise and thanksgiving, even when accompanied by complaint, protest, and petition. A call to praise, a
thanksgiving for deliverance, a series of requests accompanied by virtually any and all musical instruments and joined
by nature and heaven and all parts of the cosmos—all of this
is a part of song and prayer. This voice cries out in emotional
highs and lows, often beginning with the individual and
ending with the whole people of God, sometimes the whole
world. God—the One who delivers, who rules, who provides
direction, who is the source of wisdom, who defines right
and wrong, good and bad—is the central reference point for
this voice.

Most often this voice is found in liturgical contexts and
often associated with pedagogical intentions. For example,
in introducing and setting the tone for the book of Psalms,
Psalm 1 is, among other things, a reflective meditation, providing us with a powerful lesson on how to live well. In other
places we find prayers structured as litanies or with refrains
("Why are you cast down, O my soul . . ." occurring in Psalm
42:5, 11 and Psalm 43:5). The mood of the prayers can fluc-
tuate, from enthusiastic and emotional to contemplative and
meditative. Sometimes psalms are structured alphabetically.

This seems to some a rather pedantic and forced method of organization and expression. To others it seems testimony to an artist's creative ability.

Like the storyteller, there is no one "form" for this voice, no one topic as subject matter. But the theological orientation toward God and the voices of praise and complaint, petition, joy, and contemplation fill the Bible with powerful expressions that have a great influence on the people of God.

WHY? ROLES AND FUNCTIONS

The most obvious and most important function of the singer and pray-er biblical voice is to point to and focus on God in the midst of our human experience. This is done through praise and thanksgiving, which are always a central part of this voice's repertoire. But praise and thanksgiving often come only after thoughtful reflection, so this voice also asks us to be involved in serious theological questioning. Whether it be the classical questions of theodicy ("Such are the wicked; always at ease, they increase in riches. All in vain I have kept my heart clean and washed my hands in innocence. For all day long I have been plagued, and am punished every morning." Psalm 73:12–14); the experience of God's presence ("Where can I go from your spirit?" Psalm 139:7), or absence ("My God, my God, why have you forsaken me?" Psalm 22:1), this voice draws us into difficult questions about God made in light of our experience.

At other times the singer and pray-er pushes us to address our relationship to the institutions of nation and cult. Questions of God's relationship to Israel and to the other nations are raised regularly in prayer. In good times the kingship of God is praised and the central importance of Israel in the whole world is assumed:

> The LORD is great in Zion;
>   he is exalted over all the peoples. (Ps. 99:2)

In not so good times, God's special preference for Israel can be boldly affirmed:

> The nations are in an uproar, the kingdoms totter;
>> he utters his voice, the earth melts.
> The LORD of hosts is with us;
>> the God of Jacob is our refuge. (Ps. 46:6–7)

In very bad times, cries for restoration of the people and destruction of aggressor nations occur:

> How long, O LORD? Will you be angry forever?
>> Will your jealous wrath burn like fire?
> Pour out your anger on the nations that do not know you,
> and on the kingdoms
>> that do not call on your name.
> For they have devoured Jacob
>> and laid waste his habitation. (Ps. 79:5–7)

Finally, many of the songs and prayers of the Bible are individual in focus, origin, and appeal, propelling us as readers and conversation partners to examine our own lives with the same scrutiny. They urge us to take seriously the same difficult and perennial questions and issues.

Another function of the voice of singing and praying is to raise the issue of complaint, mostly complaint to and about God. Promises made by God to the people have been delayed, ignored, or overlooked perhaps? In any case, this voice brings all these concerns to God's attention, boldly asking God to get with it, to fulfill promises and commitments made. At deeper levels, questions about suffering and justice are raised, suggesting, often quite explicitly, that the system of retribution is not working. God is often perceived to be absent or inactive in the midst of crises, with enemies winning and the wicked prospering.

In good times and bad, the singers and pray-ers remind themselves and others that there is a relationship between the people and God, with obligations on both sides. This affirmation and reminder ties the voice of song and prayer to the biblical voices of storyteller, lawgiver, and prophet. The final reminder of this voice is the bottom line of all prayer and song: praise, however difficult to articulate.

The voice of singer and pray-er is also a voice of consciousness-raising, prompting us to recall the things we need to complain about or praise God for. Indeed, as the prayer in Psalm 138 reminds us, our prayer and supplication are directly related to our asking for God's protection and deliverance.

The voice of singer and pray-er fulfills many important roles. This voice can be a leader and director in our worship and meditation. The praying and singing voice can act as a warm-up coach, preparing us to share our praise, our anger, our puzzlement with each other and with God in new ways. This voice can function as a spiritual director, encouraging us to adopt a rule of life filled with regular prayer and reflection, integrating faith and practice in the midst of difficult times and challenges.

Finally, the voice of song and prayer sometimes assumes the role of storyteller, albeit in new and different ways. Whatever else the songs of four special women—Miriam, Deborah, Hannah, and Mary—are doing in the Bible and in our contemporary communities of faith, they are retelling the stories of the exodus, of tribal war and victory, of special revelations, and of children. These retellings call us to the same: singing and praying the stories of ancient Israel in new ways.

WHERE? THE SIGNIFICANCE OF PLACE

In Torah, Gospels, and Prophets, we find songs and prayers attributed to some of the most significant biblical characters.

Mary, Hannah, Deborah, Moses, David, Jeremiah, and many more raise the voice of prayer and song. We may suppose that the prayers and songs associated with these figures eventually became a part of scripture by first finding their way into collections of similar writings. So, for example, the prayers of David become a part of many local collections that ultimately were combined into what became the book of Psalms.

These prayers and songs identify and heighten the role of David, as singer and pray-er; of Hannah, as recipient of God's blessing through the birth of Samuel; of Mary, as the vehicle of God's grace to the whole world, through Jesus; of Jeremiah, as a prophet who must complain about a difficult vocation while remaining faithful to the One who calls him. These central characters are seen as great examples for faithful prayer and song, thus becoming exemplars for others as well.

The biblical voice of pray-er and singer is most often found in the Writings of the Hebrew Bible. This is not accidental, but an indication of its role and function within the community of faith that shapes scripture. It is the collections of prayers and songs found in Psalms and Lamentations that usually lift up this voice in the Writings. Here one can find virtually all kinds of prayer, for virtually all occasions, with heavy emotion or calm meditation, with anger and frustration or humble acceptance, with accusations of God's injustice or attributions of God's loving-kindness shown to all.

In Psalms and Lamentations, the voice of song and prayer is clearly responding to the challenges and opportunities, the crises and great blessings regularly experienced by the people of God. Torah and Prophets, Gospels and Epistles provide the framework for understanding all of these experiences. Therefore it is hardly surprising to see constant references to the foundational stories of Torah in the Psalms and to see the many ways in which Torah helps to shape expectations of living for those in New Testament communities of faith, then and now.

Psalms and Lamentations witness to the institutionalization of prayer and song. Now we are all to use the prayers of individuals, for they are a part of the prayer and song repertoire for the whole community of faith. The institution uses these prayers and songs to remember, advocate, and sustain.

It is important to note that in the New Testament, when the voice of prayer and song is cited, it is almost always in a prophetic manner. That is, the voice confirms that something has happened already foretold in scripture. This is an interesting development, which entails looking at all scripture not solely in terms of its ostensible function and voice, but as potentially imparting a prophetic dimension and intention.

SO WHAT? SHAPING CONVERSATION

Virtually all proponents of spirituality (or spiritual growth, formation, nurture, or whatever other term we use to signify our relationship with the Other) lift up the role of prayer and song as central to the development of that relationship. Put another way, whether we are talking about the prayer of Jesus in Gethsemane before the crucifixion, or David's song of praise at the end of many stories of his exploits, or the song of Deborah, or the *Magnificat* of Mary, these prayers are more than material for the historian or biographer, they are voices intended to shape us in our relationship with God and, often, with each other.

Remember one of the primary functions of this voice: to tie God to everything we experience, to take God seriously. The Writings, with their normative and referential nature, demand that we do this! David was a man of prayer, and so must we be! Mary was a special vehicle of God's grace, and so must we be! The psalmists were unafraid to ask big things of God, to remind God of promises made and not yet fulfilled, to complain about harsh treatment at the hands of enemies. So must we be! The voice of prayer and song shapes us, urging us to bring all of our lives into a context of worship.

We are encouraged to see the pertinence of old news (like things recounted in the Bible), of old struggles (like the exodus, like the adventures of Paul and Barnabas), not as history but as applicable to our lives right now. The voice of song and prayer, through our interrelationship with it, becomes a means of community memory, of community encouragement, of community relationship development. More than any other voice in the Bible, the voice of prayer and song says: Go and do likewise!

All of this brings us to the voice of the lawgiver, who speaks of both the detail of going to do likewise, as well as the rationale for it: covenant relationship with a God who has delivered from oppression and death to freedom and new life.

STUDY QUESTIONS

Pick a favorite biblical prayer or song (or maybe two, one Old Testament and one New Testament), and briefly describe this voice by providing some answers to the following questions[1]:

- *What? Recognizing the Voice (Content and Form)*. What does the voice of the singer or pray-er that you have chosen look like?
- *Why? Roles and Functions (Intention)*. What is the agenda of the singer or pray-er in this text? Why is this text written and passed down to us?
- *Where? The Significance of Place (Setting and Canonical View)*. In what particular part of scripture is this song or prayer found? How does this placement add to its meaning?

---

1. For a fuller set of questions on these subjects, see the Introduction (pp. x–xii).

- *So What? Shaping Conversation (Application of Agenda;
  Formation).* Think of a situation in which this particular
  biblical voice might be especially valuable. What does a
  good conversation with this voice for the situation you
  have chosen look like? What positive things might this
  voice suggest? What new things might the voice suggest?
  Things you weren't necessarily looking for or maybe
  don't even want, but this voice wants factored in. . . .

5

TALKING WITH THE BIBLE AS LAWGIVER

EXODUS 19:3–8

Then Moses went up to God; the LORD called to him from the mountain, saying, "Thus you shall say to the house of Jacob, and tell the Israelites: You have seen what I did to the Egyptians, and how I bore you on eagles' wings and brought you to myself. Now therefore, if you obey my voice and keep my covenant, you shall be my treasured possession out of all the peoples. Indeed, the whole earth is mine, but you shall be for me a priestly kingdom and a holy nation. These are the words that you shall speak to the Israelites."

So Moses came, summoned the elders of the people, and set before them all these words that the LORD had commanded him. The people all answered as one: "Everything that the LORD has spoken we will do." Moses reported the words of the people to the LORD.

LEVITICUS 19:1–8

The LORD spoke to Moses, saying:

Speak to all the congregation of the people of Israel and say to them: You shall be holy, for I the LORD your God am holy. You shall each revere your mother and father, and you shall keep my sabbaths: I am the LORD your God. Do not turn to idols or make cast images for yourselves: I am the LORD your God.

When you offer a sacrifice of well-being to the LORD, offer it in such a way that it is acceptable on your behalf. It shall be eaten on the same day you offer it, or on the next day; and anything left over until the third day shall be consumed in fire. If it is eaten at all on the third day, it is an abomination; it will not be acceptable. All who eat it shall be subject to punishment, because they have profaned what is holy to the LORD; and any such person shall be cut off from the people.

MATTHEW 5:1–12

When Jesus saw the crowds, he went up the mountain; and after he sat down, his disciples came to him. Then he began to speak, and taught them, saying:

"Blessed are the poor in spirit, for theirs is the kingdom of heaven.

"Blessed are those who mourn, for they will be comforted.

"Blessed are the meek, for they will inherit the earth.

"Blessed are those who hunger and thirst for righteousness, for they will be filled.

"Blessed are the merciful, for they will receive mercy.

"Blessed are the pure in heart, for they will see God.

"Blessed are the peacemakers, for they will be called children of God.

"Blessed are those who are persecuted for righteousness' sake, for theirs is the kingdom of heaven.

"Blessed are you when people revile you and persecute you and utter all kinds of evil against you falsely on my account. Rejoice and be glad, for your reward is great in heaven, for in the same way they persecuted the prophets who were before you."

1 PETER 1:13–23

Therefore prepare your minds for action; discipline yourselves; set all your hope on the grace that Jesus Christ will
bring you when he is revealed. Like obedient children, do
not be conformed to the desires that you formerly had in
ignorance. Instead, as he who called you is holy, be holy
yourselves in all your conduct; for it is written, "You shall
be holy, for I am holy."

If you invoke as Father the one who judges all people
impartially according to their deeds, live in reverent fear
during the time of your exile. You know that you were ran-
somed from the futile ways inherited from your ancestors,
not with perishable things like silver or gold, but with the
precious blood of Christ, like that of a lamb without defect
or blemish. He was destined before the foundation of the
world, but was revealed at the end of the ages for your sake.
Through him you have come to trust in God, who raised
him from the dead and gave him glory, so that your faith
and hope are set on God.

Now that you have purified your souls by your obedience
to the truth so that you have genuine mutual love, love one
another deeply from the heart. You have been born anew,
not of perishable but of imperishable seed, through the living and enduring word of God.

WHAT? RECOGNIZING THE VOICE

Our first two scriptural voices calling us into conversation
with the Bible were primary voices. A strong case could be
made that both the storyteller and the singer and pray-er are
among the first to speak in the Bible. Such is not the case
for the lawgiver. The voice of the lawgiver grows out of a
relationship in the process of developing. It is grounded in
specific events, the significance of which will be addressed by
the lawgiver. In Exodus 19, for example, the giving of the law

follows an invitation into a relationship created by the exodus of the people by God. The people are actually given a choice: ". . . therefore, if you obey my voice and keep my covenant, you shall be my treasured possession out of all the peoples." Presumably, then, the people could have said: "Thanks, but no thanks, we'll go it on our own from here." Put another way, entering into a relationship with consequences and responsibilities requires an intentional act of commitment. That commitment comes *prior* to the voice of the lawgiver and is based on the specific acts we have heard in the voices of storytellers and singers.

How will we recognize the voice of the lawgiver? Much of this voice comes cloaked with legal and moral rhetoric, so words like "justice," "judgment," "loans," "pledges," "witnesses," "statutes," "ordinances," or "law" are all good indicators we may be hearing the voice of the lawgiver. Laws are for groups—for families or clans or peoples—so "we" is a focus. Law is a communal endeavor, given for the sake of the whole body. The relationship between God and the people is most often defined and referred to as covenant, to which legal terminology is frequently related. Because of the special character of the Bible's lawgiving, another term is often associated with this voice: holiness. Leviticus 19 exhorts: "Speak to all the congregation of the people of Israel and say to them: You shall be holy, for I the LORD your God am holy." The actual laws in the Bible, like laws in all communities, cover virtually everything. There is a great deal of attention to cultic, religious law, which, given the character of the scriptures they reside in, is hardly surprising. But there are also laws about civil matters such as property and living well with neighbors, about family, clan, or tribe, about wrongful death, and so on. The biblical voice of lawgiver is often moral in tone, leaving no room for doubt about what the consequences of disobedience to the laws will be.

If law in the Bible is marked by variety, the forms these laws take are relatively limited. Much law is marked by the imperative voice, either in terms of commands ("You shall love your mother and father") or prohibitions ("Do not turn to idols or make cast images for yourselves"). There is also a fair amount of what we might today call case law, where some of the extenuating circumstances are considered ("When you offer a sacrifice of well-being to the LORD, offer it in such a way that it is acceptable on your behalf. It shall be eaten on the same day you offer it, or on the next day; and anything left over until the third day shall be consumed in fire. If it is eaten at all on the third day, it is an abomination; it will not be acceptable").

Many laws in the Bible, particularly in Torah, are contained in speeches of God to Moses. Jesus's Sermon on the Mount in Matthew's gospel is similar. This establishes at least two important patterns. First, the ultimate lawgiver is God. Second, this voice is associated with prophets and other leaders who have special relationships with God and who carry this legal message to the people. Quite often the voice of the lawgiver is heard in the context of a theophany, a special appearance of God, which simply emphasizes the issues of origin, authority, and relationship so often associated with the law.

Biblical laws, like contemporary laws, are quite often gathered into codes or other collections, where certain types of law provide the rationale for organization. The organization of the cult, the sacrificial schedule, family relationships, calendars of worship obligations, and property issues (slaves, land, etc.) all have collections of law associated with them.

The biblical voice of the lawgiver, speaking out of the deep relationship of covenant, often uses the style and rhetoric of exhortation. Sometimes, as in Deuteronomy, collections of law are actually framed by homiletical language. At other times, as in 1 Peter, we hear the imperative voice calling us to obedience and faithful living not in precise legal forms but rather in the context of oration and community appeal. In 1 Peter and other passages, the law, or rather the behavioral norms being emphasized in the life of the community, are inseparably intertwined with stories of salvation and the special relationships of the people with God.

WHY? ROLES AND FUNCTIONS

The voice of the lawgiver in the Bible is addressing an all-important issue: the "so what" of salvation! This is, finally, the rationale and purpose of the law. As we have seen, the story of salvation, whether described in the exodus of the Hebrew Bible or in the life, death, and resurrection of Jesus in the New Testament, creates the possibility of a new relationship between the people and God. Once that relationship exists and the people commit to it, there are some "so whats" that naturally follow. The law, most often experienced in special revelatory ways as a message from God, orders and sustains the relationship created by the saving acts of God for the people.

Presuming a committed covenantal relationship, the voice of the lawgiver wants to form the people of God. There are at least three foci in doing this. First, the law helps the people develop and sustain their relationship with God. This happens through explicit commands for faithfulness and allegiance to God first, as reflected in the Decalogue (I am the LORD your God, and you shall have no other gods before me).

Second, the voice of the lawgiver cares about our relationship with one another within the body of faith. In virtually all texts that deal with the law and normative actions resulting from our relationship with God, we hear the call to love one another, more often than not using our own salvific experiences as a gauge for how we are to live together.

Finally, and far from least, the lawgiver's voice calls us to think on the other, the foreigner, the one not a part of our faith community. Sometimes this other lives in our midst—and here the voice is ambivalent. Yes, we are to love all of the created order, but when the stranger represents a threat to our purity, to our own relationship with God, then actions that maintain the separation of who is in from who is out are mandated in law. On the other hand, sometimes we are called to find ways to live with the foreigner in peaceful and productive ways, whether in our own communities or with other "foreign" nations. In the New Testament especially, the question of conversion of the foreigner to our way of understanding and experiencing God is often a significant consideration for the lawgiver.

The texts found at the beginning of this chapter are all good examples of the roles and functions of the biblical lawgiver's voice. In Exodus 19 we hear of the walls of relationship created by the exodus experience. The lawgiver tells us who we are to be within this space and relationship. Leviticus focuses on holiness, on our set-apartness. Our holy action draws us into closer relationship with God, and this behavior helps define what we are able to do in the future. The Sermon on the Mount gives us clarity, definition, and continuity with the past as the new people of God, with our savior now calling us to perfection. The first letter of Peter, like an authoritative spiritual advisor, calls us into a life of discipline, of purity and holy living, of allegiance to God, of love for and with one another. All of this, for the author of this epistle, is grounded in the saving grace of Jesus Christ.

WHERE? THE SIGNIFICANCE OF PLACE

By far, the majority of law found in the Bible is associated with mountains and high places, most particularly Sinai. It is probably good that the exact location of this physical mountain continues to be debated. What is most significant about this mountain is that it is, as actually named by one biblical source, the mountain of God. It is a place where God has appeared, a place of experiencing God's presence, a place of theophany. This happened first for Moses, then for the people of Israel. On another mountain the crowds experienced another theophany in the teaching and preaching of Jesus, focusing on the law, both new and old. All of this mountaintop law grew out of and called for ongoing relationships between the people and God.

There are other places where we learn from the lawgiver. For example, as the communities of Ezra and Nehemiah struggled with what God intended after so many years of exile and bickering and ineffectual living, a new "Torah" enlightened and directed them. Or, in the communities founded by the apostles, new ways of living faithfully were made known.

Almost always, later developments in community living requiring new laws and rules are related to the earlier, foundational voices found in Torah and the Gospels. It is, of course, the very nature of law as a socially and temporally determined entity (in addition to whatever theological attributes we may wish to give it) to change. We can see this change already in the case law of the Old Testament, where older values and physical circumstances need revision as the people become sedentary. Indeed, the overall structure of Torah contains a paradigm for its own continuation and development. The book of Deuteronomy, the "second law," reflects the need of the people to think on new ways of living as they enter the promised land. That reflection process and the ongoing development of new law, always in line with the old law, is a central part of Torah.

SO WHAT? SHAPING CONVERSATION

The voice of the lawgiver calls us to serious conversation about formation. Whatever the character of our relationship with God, it results in a mandate for obedience and faithful living for which there are standards and expectations. The "so what" of our salvation experience does not go away. It is not merely a "pie in the sky" experience that has little or nothing to do with how we live our lives. It doesn't go away. It lays obligation upon us. The "works versus faith" debates do not soften the idea that we are to be different, shaped in special ways, as a result of hearing and listening to the lawgiver.

STUDY QUESTIONS

Pick a favorite biblical text (or maybe two, one Old Testament and one New Testament) representative of the lawgiver, and briefly describe this voice by providing some answers to the following questions[1]:

- *What? Recognizing the Voice (Content and Form).* What does the voice of the lawgiver that you have chosen look like?
- *Why? Roles and Functions (Intention).* What is the agenda of the lawgiver in this text? Why is this text written and passed down to us?
- *Where? The Significance of Place (Setting and Canonical View).* In what particular part of scripture is this story found? How does this placement add to its meaning?
- *So What? Shaping Conversation (Application of Agenda; Formation).* Think of a situation in which this particular biblical voice might be especially valuable. What does a good conversation with this voice for the situation you have chosen look like? What positive things might this voice suggest? What new things might the voice suggest? Things you weren't necessarily looking for or maybe don't even want, but this voice wants factored in. . . .

---

1. For a fuller set of questions on these subjects, see the Introduction (pp. x–xii).

6

TALKING WITH THE BIBLE AS PROPHET

DEUTERONOMY 18:17–19

Then the LORD replied to me: "They are right in what they have said. I will raise up for them a prophet like you from among their own people; I will put my words in the mouth of the prophet, who shall speak to them everything that I command. Anyone who does not heed the words that the prophet shall speak in my name, I myself will hold accountable."

MATTHEW 5:17–18

Do not think that I have come to abolish the law or the prophets; I have come not to abolish but to fulfill. For truly I tell you, until heaven and earth pass away, not one letter, not one stroke of a letter, will pass from the law until all is accomplished.

JEREMIAH 1:4–10

Now the word of the LORD came to me saying,
"Before I formed you in the womb I knew you,
    and before you were born I consecrated you;
    I appointed you a prophet to the nations."

Then I said, "Ah, Lord God! Truly I do not know how to
speak, for I am only a boy." But the Lord said to me,
"Do not say, 'I am only a boy';

> for you shall go to all to whom I send you,

> and you shall speak whatever I command you.

Do not be afraid of them,

> for I am with you to deliver you, says the Lord."

Then the Lord put out his hand and touched my mouth;
and the Lord said to me,
"Now I have put my words in your mouth.
See, today I appoint you over nations and over kingdoms,

> to pluck up and to pull down,

> to destroy and to overthrow,

> to build and to plant."

LUKE 4:16–21

When he came to Nazareth, where he had been brought up,
he went to the synagogue on the sabbath day, as was his
custom. He stood up to read, and the scroll of the prophet
Isaiah was given to him. He unrolled the scroll and found
the place where it was written:

"The Spirit of the Lord is upon me,
because he has anointed me to bring good news to the poor.
He has sent me to proclaim release to the captives
and recovery of sight to the blind,
to let the oppressed go free,
to proclaim the year of the Lord's favor."

And he rolled up the scroll, gave it back to the attendant,
and sat down. The eyes of all in the synagogue were fixed
on him. Then he began to say to them, "Today this scripture
has been fulfilled in your hearing."

WHAT? RECOGNIZING THE VOICE

There are many different kinds of prophetic voices in the Bible, but they all share the mission to be messenger of God. Most often this message is intended for the whole people, but sometimes it is directed to kings or other leaders. The prophetic voice is usually very well informed. Prophets would be readers of newspapers and other information sources today. The prophets were often strategically placed in or near the major institutions of their day: the court, the cult, the palace, the armies, and the intersection between the states of Israel and Judah and the surrounding nations.

The voice of the prophet is found in a variety of literary forms. We have many prose narratives about prophets in the Hebrew Bible found in the books of Jonah, Jeremiah, Ezekiel, and Isaiah, among others. Sometimes, as in the case of Jeremiah, there is a biographical recounting of events concerning the prophet. At other times, and Jonah is a good example of this, we have almost a legend or story-like quality to the writing, with the life and exploits of the prophet carrying the message of the book, rather than oracles from the prophet himself. Prose passages in the Hebrew Prophets can also reflect later interpretations of originally poetic messages. These can be important parts of the overall prophetic voice in the Bible.

By far the most common form for the prophetic voice, however, is the oracle: a message straight from God through the mouth of the prophet, and most often in poetry. Even here, however, major exceptions must be noted, such as the long oracular prose chapters attributed to Ezekiel. Prophetic oracles are usually easy to identify. They often begin with the characteristic messenger formula "Thus says the Lord." They are often punctuated with the short "says the Lord" or "a saying of the Lord."

The subject matter of the prophet is wide ranging, but judgment, promise, destruction, and restoration are common themes. Though the prophet is much more a preacher than a predictor of future events, the powerful—sometimes to the point of being offensive and difficult to hear—messages of the prophetic voices are rarely equivocal, but point to clear problems and solutions. Cries for social justice abound in the Prophets, as do critiques and scathing assessments of the cult and clergy. Many prophetic voices speak of a call from God as their reason for proclamation—and their willingness to alienate and judge others. In all of these messages there are references to the covenant, to the law, to the religious and political establishment, priests and kings. The prophet uses a powerful vocabulary and rhetorical style. There are imperatives in prophetic speech, commanding us to listen, to look, to wake up, to see the blindingly obvious. The prophet uses language to grab our attention: "Behold," "therefore," "woe," and "because" are strewn throughout the oracles, seeking our understanding, focus, and repentance. Sometimes, of course, it is already too late, but before we actually experience the death determined for us because of sin and disobedience, the prophet seeks our understanding of our shortcomings.

WHY? ROLES AND FUNCTIONS

If the voice of the lawgiver presupposes earlier stories, songs, and prayers, the prophet does so even more. A conversation with the Bible as prophet depends upon and presupposes a relationship between God and the people of Israel. The prophet is not speaking for him or herself, but for God, and the message is not coming from out of the blue. The voice of the lawgiver is a huge presupposition for the prophet: there *is* a "so what" to the relationship between people and God. The words of both singer/pray-er and storyteller are also often cited by the prophet. The prophet knows the importance of worship in the life of the people and grounds the communal identity in the classic stories of patriarchs, kings, salvific events, and sacred places.

In our passage from Deuteronomy, Moses, lawgiver *par excellence*, becomes the paradigm for all prophets. In many ways Moses is the ideal prophet, for he surely has more direct messages for the people than any other biblical figure. It is clear enough that Jeremiah's call models Moses's, thus authenticating and authorizing Jeremiah's own prophetic message and ministry. Jesus again affirms the validity and value of that Mosaic message in the Gospel of Matthew, even as Luke gives Jesus the role of prophetic interpretation and implementation in our passage from Luke 4.

The prophet usually announces and proclaims the message from God in dramatic fashion. More often than not, the message appears to come as a surprise to its recipient and is often not embraced or welcomed warmly. There is, then, an informational aspect to the prophetic voice. The prophet wants us to see what is really happening in the world through this message.

The prophetic voice often starts with a word of judgment. Things are not going well, the message tends to acknowledge. Maybe the people and the king knew this was true, maybe not. But, from God's perspective, the covenant relationship has been violated, and a message of judgment with consequences is required. Sometimes the people are ridiculed or accused of many horrible sins. Sometimes the enemies of the people assume the role of implementer of judgment, rubbing salt into wounds. Sometimes the people seem unaware of how poorly they have abided by covenant promises and stipulations. When this happens there is often very strong language used to judge them.

One presupposition common to all prophetic messages is that God is ultimately in control. There are consequences for being disobedient and dismissive of the covenantal relationship.

Sometimes the king and other leaders or teachers are the "bad guys" who will bear these consequences. But the later voices of prophets increasingly assume that the whole people of God will bear the costs of outrageous behavior, whether they have actually participated or not. In light of all this, there may or may not be hope for the future. Sometimes there are wonderful visions of restoration and rejuvenation of the people, sometimes not. But restoration already presupposes a loss, a destruction, a severe judgment. Even one of the most hopeful of the prophets, Isaiah, says that Jerusalem and the people have "received from the Lord's hand double for all her sins" (40:2). In all of this the prophet is mixing old and new. The new can be a judgment with a death sentence or a promise of restoration. But the new is always dependent upon the old, and often uses the language of the old to speak of new things. The reference of Jeremiah to the "new" actions of God for the people is a good example:

> Therefore, the days are surely coming, says the LORD, when it shall no longer be said, "As the LORD lives who brought the people of Israel up out of the land of Egypt," but "As the LORD lives who brought out and led the offspring of the house of Israel out of the land of the north and out of all the lands where he had driven them." Then they shall live in their own land. (Jer. 23:7–8)

The voice of the Bible as prophet fulfills several functions. It is a constant reminder that we live in a theological world. We may or may not choose to acknowledge this and to act accordingly, but the prophet presupposes such a world and a God who still speaks. The voice of the prophet provides a reality check for the people of God. Whether we want it or not, whether we agree with it or not, the prophet gives us a theological message about the state of the world and our responsibility and culpability for it. The voice of the prophet offers a corrective to our actions. More often than not, this corrective is based on the voice and message of the lawgiver. So the prophetic voice also reminds and calls us back to old commitments. Finally, the voice of the prophet speaks of a continuum between old and new, demanding that the people acknowledge and live into this continuum.

WHERE? THE SIGNIFICANCE OF PLACE

The voice of the prophet is associated with the significant institutions in biblical times. There are prophets in the cult, sometimes prophesying to the people in public, sometimes giving oracles in the context of worship. There are prophets at the palace, providing advice to kings and other high-ranking government officials. There are prophetic guilds, often arranged and propagated through family lines, providing advice and direction to clans, tribal leaders, or kings. Some of these prophets are actually employed by the institutions, creating a potential conflict of interest should the message they receive be at odds with the welfare of the cult or monarchy. Perhaps this is why the Bible often speaks of this type of prophet with disdain (Nathan is a notable exception), equating their message and role with the organization's own misguided message and mission.

Institutional employment was not the norm for prophets. Indeed, many prophets appear to be totally independent, called by God to deliver particular messages and then, as far as we can tell, returning to whatever they were doing before called. The most significant point about place and prophet is that prophets find a way to be right in the middle of the institutions to which they will speak.

Not surprisingly, most of the prophetic voices in the Bible are located in the canonical section that bears their name, Prophets. Although there is clearly a waning of prophecy by the time of the New Testament, the voice can still be heard.

As we have argued, the Epistles of the New Testament have significant parallels with the Prophets in the Hebrew Bible. However, with the development of a literary canon, there is no doubt the phenomenon of prophecy is changing. The Prophets are now books to be read to the people. The analogy for the writings of the apostles (epistles read to the gathered community of Christians) is clear. All of this will result in fewer prophets, on the one hand, and a prophetic interpretation of already extant scripture, on the other. So, for example, if we find ways to apply the message of the Psalms to our contemporary life, we might well begin to consider its traditional author, David, as a prophet! This pattern occurs many times in the New Testament.

As our text from Deuteronomy makes clear, however, Torah is the bedrock for prophecy, as it contains the first and primary covenants between Israel and God. Without this relationship, the prophetic messages have no traction, no credibility. If Torah is the ground upon which prophecy stands, it also provides the model for a prophet, namely Moses, the messenger of God *par excellence*! In the New Testament, while Torah still provides the bedrock for a prophetic voice, it is now Jesus who defines what prophecy must look like. Jesus does this by his own actions, as exemplified in the synagogue experience recounted by Luke, where his particular interpretative action and words become the norm for subsequent use of the prophetic voice. Moreover, the salvific work accomplished in and by Jesus forms the centerpiece of the apostolic message in the Epistles and all the New Testament.

SO WHAT? SHAPING CONVERSATION

In one real sense, the Bible has tamed the prophet. Rather than an often emotional presence delivering vitriolic and difficult judgments, we have a text that can be ignored. What this really means is that we will probably find it a difficult proposition to have a significant conversation with the prophetic voice of the Bible. Unless, however, we assume that we would never be the subject of a prophet's scorn and indictment!

The prophetic voice in the Bible calls us to stop what we are doing and to listen. Just as important, the prophet calls us to reflect on what is happening in our lives and in the world. Often, on the basis of these two actions, we are asked to turn around, to go in a different direction, a direction very often different from where the establishment is going, doing things very different from what the establishment is doing. Not all of us are introspective, but the prophetic voice ultimately asks us to be.

Our contemporary relationship with the prophetic voice is to use it as a barometer for how well we work for social justice. If we care about all of this, if we say the right things and give the right money to the right organizations, then we will be in good shape. We may even congratulate ourselves for being in such close touch with our prophet friends and actually see our own ministries as prophetic as well.

At the risk of offending, when we speak positively about the prophets in the Bible and equate their messages with our churches and their voices, I think we are often being facile and, probably, wildly inaccurate. First of all, the prophets did not mince words. Most of them spoke harshly. They were intolerant of good intentions not followed by radical actions. They are not good conversation partners, as they really don't want to hear what we have to say. In one sense, then, there is little that is dialogical about the prophets. They are telling us what we have done and what we need to do if we want to live well or live at all. To talk with them is fundamentally to listen to them, to ask for clarity so that we can perform the radical assessment of our churches. I have no doubt the prophets have much to say about the decline of the church and about its not-so-promising future. All of this, if the prophets are to be true to their voices in the Bible, will be talk about death, about change, about turning around. Conversation around topics like this is critical for our future, but not necessarily pleasant or easy.

STUDY QUESTIONS

Pick a favorite biblical text (or maybe two, one Old Testament and one New Testament) representative of the prophet, and briefly describe this voice by providing some answers to the following questions[1]:

- *What? Recognizing the Voice (Content and Form).* What does the voice of the prophet that you have chosen look like?

- *Why? Roles and Functions (Intention).* What is the agenda of the prophet in this text? Why is this text written and passed down to us?

- *Where? The Significance of Place (Setting and Canonical View).* In what particular part of scripture is this story found? How does this placement add to its meaning?

- *So What? Shaping Conversation (Application of Agenda; Formation).* Think of a situation in which this particular biblical voice might be especially valuable. What does a good conversation with this voice for the situation you have chosen look like? What positive things might this voice suggest? What new things might the voice suggest? Things you weren't necessarily looking for or maybe don't even want, but this voice wants factored in. . . .

---

1. For a fuller set of questions on these subjects, see the Introduction (pp. x–xii).

TALKING WITH THE BIBLE AS HISTORIAN

GENESIS 1:1–5

In the beginning when God created the heavens and the earth, the earth was a formless void and darkness covered the face of the deep, while a wind from God swept over the face of the waters. Then God said, "Let there be light"; and there was light. And God saw that the light was good; and God separated the light from the darkness. God called the light Day, and the darkness he called Night. And there was evening and there was morning, the first day.

JOHN 1:1–5

In the beginning was the Word, and the Word was with God, and the Word was God. He was in the beginning with God. All things came into being through him, and without him not one thing came into being. What has come into being in him was life, and the life was the light of all people. The light shines in the darkness, and the darkness did not overcome it.

1 KINGS 2:1–4

When David's time to die drew near, he charged his son Solomon, saying: "I am about to go the way of all the earth.

Be strong, be courageous, and keep the charge of the LORD your God, walking in his ways and keeping his statutes, his commandments, his ordinances, and his testimonies, as it is written in the law of Moses, so that you may prosper in all that you do and wherever you turn. Then the LORD will establish his word that he spoke concerning me: 'If your heirs take heed to their way, to walk before me in faithfulness with all their heart and with all their soul, there shall not fail you a successor on the throne of Israel.'"

1 CHRONICLES 29:26–30

Thus David son of Jesse reigned over all Israel. The period that he reigned over Israel was forty years; he reigned for seven years in Hebron, and thirty-three years in Jerusalem. He died in a good old age, full of days, riches, and honor; and his son Solomon succeeded him. Now the acts of King David, from first to last, are written in the records of the seer Samuel, and in the records of the prophet Nathan, and in the records of the seer Gad, with accounts of all his rule and his might and of the events that befell him and Israel and all the kingdoms of the earth.

2 CHRONICLES 36:9–10

Jehoiachin was eight years old when he began to reign; he reigned for three months and ten days in Jerusalem. He did what was evil in the sight of the LORD. In the spring of the year King Nebuchadnezzar sent and brought him to Babylon, along with the precious vessels of the house of the LORD, and made his brother Zedekiah king over Judah and Jerusalem.

ACTS 28:30–31

[Paul] lived there for two whole years at his own expense and welcomed all who came to him, proclaiming the kingdom of God and teaching about the Lord Jesus Christ with all boldness and without hindrance.

WHAT? RECOGNIZING THE VOICE

At first glance there seems to be a lot of similarity between the Bible as storyteller and the Bible as historian. Short stories, such as the story of Abraham and Sarah in Genesis or any of the stories of Jesus and his healing miracles in the Gospels, are relatively easy to identify and recognize. When those stories are gathered into larger complexes, they are often labeled "history." It behooves us, therefore, to spend a little time attempting to distinguish between these two voices of the Bible.

The beginning verses of Genesis and John epitomize the challenges before us. The Genesis text can be seen as the introduction to an originally independent creation account that ends in the first few verses of the second chapter of Genesis. It can also be the introduction to the so-called prehistory of Genesis, encompassing the first eleven chapters of that book. Or it can be the introduction to the whole book of Genesis, or to Torah, or to the whole Bible. Likewise, the opening verses of John can be seen as the introduction to the so-called prologue of the gospel. As such these verses are part of a short section able to stand alone or they are a part of a larger introduction to the whole gospel.

Many students of the Bible have labeled the larger literary entities to which Genesis 1:1–5 or John 1:1–5 belong as "history." But surely this history is different from, for example, the history of the people of Israel and Judah we find in 1–2 Kings or 1–2 Chronicles or the history of the early church we find in the book of Acts. And all of this "history" is very different from any contemporary critical definition of that activity. Indeed, if we use contemporary definitions of history and historians as our guides, then there is no history in the Bible. This is very different from saying we can't read the Bible historically. However, to read the Bible from the perspective of a contemporary understanding of history is to engage in a very different kind of conversation, a conversation that is controlled by factors never in the minds of those who composed the Bible or who wrote, for example, either Genesis 1:1–5 or John 1:1–5.

The issue before us is fairly straightforward. If we want to have a conversation with the Bible as historian, then we will need to listen to it and hear it on its own terms. To do this involves seeing at least two kinds of "history" in the Bible. The history we find beginning with Genesis 1 or John 1 has often been called *Heilsgeschichte* or Salvation History. It is a big-picture view of the interrelationship of God and humanity in the context of the created order that entails the tying together of smaller stories and other biblical literature (for example, genealogies, prayer and songs, itineraries) to create the larger entity. This process continues even after the completion of the Bible, up to the present day.

The other kind of history we find in the Bible looks much more like contemporary history than Genesis or the Gospel of John. It is the history found in the books of Samuel, Kings, Chronicles, Ezra, Nehemiah, and Acts. As in Genesis, there are stories about individuals which represent the majority of the source material. However, it is the focus on institutions, namely the kingdoms of Israel and Judah or the early church, that controls the overall literary presentation and its use of other, non-story materials. A good illustration of the difference between storyteller and historian in the Bible can be found by comparing the story of covenant with Abram in Genesis 15 with the story we find in 2 Samuel 7. In many ways the covenant is the same: a relationship created through the promise of God to patriarch or king, where acknowledgment and acceptance of the promise by its recipient are all that is necessary. The result is the gift of land with approximately the same borders in Genesis and Samuel. Both of these stories, however, are parts of much larger literary entities. Both of them include other records and resources, which create a bigger picture. The account in 2 Samuel 7 brings in another kind of obligatory covenant, most often associated with Moses and Sinai, even though the overall validity of the promise of a house forever remains. In Genesis we will wait a few more chapters before hearing still one more covenant story that features the obligatory version of relationship between God and the people (Genesis 17).

When the stories that form the basis of Genesis 15 and 2 Samuel 7 are compared, however, some significant differences appear. The scope of 2 Samuel 7 is much larger. There is more detail and more attention to the larger history to which this story belongs. Moreover, the historian in 2 Samuel uses more materials and records to tell the story. In contrast, the story of Abram found in Genesis 15, though part of a larger whole, reads as if it were complete in itself, a story that could be told over and over again as an example of Abram's special relationship with God and of the promises made to the patriarch. The story of David and the promise made to him about his house is much more fully integrated into the stories and other materials that precede and follow this text. 2 Samuel 7 is filled with lots of interpretative activity—expanding and nuancing and making it more than just a story, making it start to look like a history of David and his reign.

So, while in Genesis we have a larger complex of stories combined to create a salvation history, we also have a more official institutional history in Samuel. This institutional history still uses stories, still speaks of God's active presence in the life of the state, its leaders, and people, but it reads very differently than the stories found in Genesis.

Talking with the Bible as historian will focus on the more explicit institutional texts in scripture, leaving the other history to the voice of the storyteller.

WHY? ROLES AND FUNCTIONS

The most clearly recognizable characteristic of the Bible as historian, namely its explicit concern for institutional life, is also the key to its role and function within the Bible. Three explicit histories in the Bible care deeply about the monarchy and state, the cult, and the early church: Samuel–Kings; Chronicles, Ezra, and Nehemiah; Acts. Though we know little about the authors of these works, it is safe to say they are builders or administrators of these institutions and deeply committed to them. These histories usually have a conservative bias. They care about the maintenance of the institution and are often invested in the status quo, in what will make the monarchy, cult, or church, to use a modern word, sustainable. In accomplishing this, these histories focus on those things critical for the efficient running of the institutions they describe. Stories about clergy, kings, prophets, worship and the temple, and the palace are placed within the history in ways that enhance a particular interpretation of the institution. Even when the institution is in trouble, as is surely the case in much of the history of Israel and Judah found in Samuel, Kings, Chronicles, Ezra, and Nehemiah, the monarchy or the cult is lifted up as a continuing vehicle for God's relationship with the people, albeit with a bit of exile and difficulty along the way.

Biblical historians take seriously the records and stories of the past but also seek to set forth new ways in which to interpret them in light of constantly changing challenges. In the case of the history found in the books of Chronicles, we also have a revisionist motive, otherwise it's hard to understand why the history was written at all. The pictures of David and Solomon, for example, are very different in these two histories. David is a brilliant and charismatic, but flawed leader in Samuel. On his death bed he warns Solomon to be faithful to the laws and statutes in order to live successfully into the promises God has for the monarchy and state. In Chronicles, David has accomplished, or set in motion, virtually all the things Solomon does in Kings, so on his death bed there is no need to admonish Solomon, for everything is in place.

There is also a significant parallel between Chronicles and Acts, which points to the open-endedness of these histories. In both books we find central figures (Jehoiachin, king of Judah, and the apostle Paul, respectively) under house arrest. This leaves both histories open to questions about the future, especially how the people will fare under foreign domination. Here the social, political, and theological are combined into powerful messages for later communities.

WHERE? THE SIGNIFICANCE OF PLACE

One significant element of the large complexes of stories melded together in Torah and the Gospels is their confessional and foundational character. This character is the basis for identity and for mission. The histories of the people that we find in the Former Prophets (Joshua, Judges, 1–2 Samuel, 1–2 Kings), the Writings, and the New Testament bounce off these foundations, accept the contours of relationship and obligation presented there, and tell a part of the subsequent life of Israel and the New Israel. It is important to understand that all of these histories must be interpreted in light of Torah and the Gospels.

Though the history of Israel and Judah is one of ups and downs, the ultimate picture is a damning judgment of monarchy, cult, and people—with the loss of every major institution and ultimate subservience to foreign powers. The history bounces off of and traces the fortunes of Israel and Judah in light of the call for covenant obedience in Torah. It is a history filled with failure and triumph, with sin and faithfulness, with catastrophe and great accomplishment. All of this is tied together with a series of prophecy-fulfillment events, which illustrate the truth of Torah and the consequences of forsaking covenant obligations. The question of the future is left open, but is not particularly positive. Here, then, the voice of the prophet is integrated into a history affirming the import of that special word throughout a significant part of the people's history.

We have a very different picture in the Writings. The history of what has happened cannot be erased; but we can talk about how we will continue to live and be faithful in light of such grim judgments and experiences. It is time, if you will, to rewrite the history of the people, to shape it in order to lift up new, hopefully positive, ways to move forward. Thus the Chronicler (1–2 Chronicles, Ezra, Nehemiah) will stress the positive whenever possible. David will continue to be a paradigm for the future. But in a time when there is no monarchy, it is important to stress the activities of David that the people can emulate and develop more fully, while still hoping for better things. So David becomes a community builder, a designer of the Temple, a vehicle for present work, as well as the basis for future actions of God, through a messiah, in the future. Because the Chronicler is writing after the exile, the history is extended to include Ezra and Nehemiah, lifting up the centrality of Torah, making the cult the central infrastructure for society, and facing questions of identity and mission in a land no longer under the control of Israel.

In the New Testament, the history of the early church recounted in Acts represents a bit of both the Former Prophets and the Chronicler. It begins with the new, post-Gospel, starting point: the resurrection of Jesus. As such, it needs to deal first with Jesus's post-resurrection presence, his leaving, and the coming of the Holy Spirit, all beginning points of great significance for the early church. The early history of this institution also includes the roles and adventures of Peter, Paul, and the other early disciples and apostles found in this book. What is not new to this particular history are the ups and downs of the people, the infighting, the different visions of community, evangelism, and mission. These are issues and concerns for all historians in the Bible.

The historian in the Bible calls us to remember and learn from our history, a history we often repeat. The historians in Former Prophets call us to turn around and repent. The historians in Chronicles ask us to consider the task of community builders, of centrality of scripture (Torah), of accommodation with foreign powers. The historians in Acts proclaim the newness of Jesus, even as that history notes that the ways we articulate and live out his significance differ widely.

SO WHAT? SHAPING CONVERSATION

What does a conversation with a biblical historian look like? First, and perhaps most importantly, any conversation with a historian will have a prophetic dimension. We will be asked to remember our past and to be open to changing. This, of course, is based on the premise that we are prone to forget our past, to forget some of the foundational points in our relationship with one another and with God. Put another way, it is not just the people of God in the Bible who are messed up! Rather, we all have the ability and inclination to forget, to deny, to overlook, to find the easy way out of the relational mandates and obligations that are so much a part of being God's people in the world.

On the positive side, we should be prepared to receive and act on long-standing promises to live well, to be fruitful and multiply, to create productive and happy communities of faith that serve the world with significant ministries. We are to follow the lead of the bold early historians of Israel, who saw David, Ezra, and Jesus, to name but three, leading God's people through challenge and hardship to fulfillment and restoration. To continue to do this, to engage in conversation with these historians, is to ask how the monarchy and other foundational institutions of times past will be significant in a very different world.

The Chronicler presents us with significant challenges. Yes, we will be community builders and we will search for the glue that holds our communities of faith together. Will it be a narrow definition of Torah and obedience to it that does the trick? Or will we find other interpretations of the foundational stories and canon as we explore ways to live in a world not dominated by our own communities of faith? In many ways, this question continues into the New Testament.

We are called to witness and to evangelize even as we remain mindful of inclusivity and diversity and our need to respect the thoughts and communities of the other. But even as we are called to a broad conception of mission, we are also challenged not to be afraid of argument and disagreement within our nuclear communities of faith. We must find ways to embrace and live with the universal and the particular, at one and the same time. To do this is to learn from and to have serious conversations with the historians of our biblical communities.

STUDY QUESTIONS

Pick a favorite biblical text (or maybe two, one Old Testament and one New Testament) representative of the historian, and briefly describe this voice by providing some answers to the following questions[1]:

- *What? Recognizing the Voice (Content and Form).* What does the voice of the historian that you have chosen look like?
- *Why? Roles and Functions (Intention).* What is the agenda of the historian in this text? Why is this story written and passed down to us?

---

1. For a fuller set of questions on these subjects, see the Introduction (pp. x–xii).

- *Where? The Significance of Place (Setting and Canonical View)*. In what particular part of scripture is this text found? How does this placement add to its meaning?
- *So What? Shaping Conversation (Application of Agenda; Formation)*. Think of a situation in which this particular biblical voice might be especially valuable. What does a good conversation with this voice for the situation you have chosen look like? What positive things might this voice suggest? What new things might the voice suggest? Things you weren't necessarily looking for or maybe don't even want, but this voice wants factored in. . . .

CHAPTER

8

TALKING WITH THE BIBLE AS VISIONARY

ZECHARIAH 6:1–7
And again I looked up and saw four chariots coming out from between two mountains—mountains of bronze. The first chariot had red horses, the second chariot black horses, the third chariot white horses, and the fourth chariot dappled grey horses. Then I said to the angel who talked with me, "What are these, my lord?" The angel answered me, "These are the four winds of heaven going out, after presenting themselves before the LORD of all the earth. The chariot with the black horses goes toward the north country, the white ones go toward the west country, and the dappled ones go toward the south country." When the steeds came out, they were impatient to get off and patrol the earth. And he said, "Go, patrol the earth." So they patrolled the earth.

DANIEL 7:13–16
As I watched in the night visions,
I saw one like a human being
    coming with the clouds of heaven.
And he came to the Ancient One
    and was presented before him.

To him was given dominion
>   and glory and kingship,
that all peoples, nations, and languages
>   should serve him.
His dominion is an everlasting dominion
>   that shall not pass away,
and his kingship is one
>   that shall never be destroyed.

As for me, Daniel, my spirit was troubled within me, and the visions of my head terrified me. I approached one of the attendants to ask him the truth concerning all this. So he said that he would disclose to me the interpretation of the matter. . . .

REVELATION 1:17–19

When I saw him, I fell at his feet as though dead. But he placed his right hand on me, saying, "Do not be afraid; I am the first and the last, and the living one. I was dead, and see, I am alive for ever and ever; and I have the keys of Death and of Hades. Now write what you have seen, what is, and what is to take place after this."

WHAT? RECOGNIZING THE VOICE

There is actually a lot of talk about visions in the Bible. Take, for example, the beginning of Abram's covenant with God in Genesis 15:1, "After these things the word of the LORD came to Abram in a vision. . . ." Many prophets experienced the word of God in visions. Think of the incredible vision that begins the book of Ezekiel describing God's throne and its environs! A look at key words like vision or dream will lift up a host of experiences and descriptions that can rightly be called visionary. Our concern is with special visions that set forth alternative views of the world, glimpses into a future that attempt to resolve present conflict or misunderstanding concerning God's people and the world.

While there is no particular language or style that identifies this kind of vision, there are some characteristics shared by most visionary voices in the Bible. First, and perhaps most important, the visionary voice of scripture thinks and speaks in polarities. Good and bad, right and wrong, us and them, foreign and part of the community, black and white, war and peace, day and night, life and death, universal and particular—these dramatic polarities are often at the heart of the visionary voice.

Daniel and Revelation, for example, set forth visions that are very hard to understand. Yes, it is clear what Daniel and John are seeing. No, it is not clear what the vision represents, what it means. These visions are beyond our comprehension and beyond the comprehension of the receiver of the vision as well.

There are some common topics or themes associated with these visions. War and conflict are very frequently the subject of these visions. Musing upon the fate of the good guys and the bad guys at the end of it all is also common. The desire of the person who has the vision (such as John or Daniel) to understand what it means and what application it might have for contemporary faith and living is also a regular part of these types of visions. Many of these visions have the form of an apocalypse, a vision of end times. Though the content of such visions is not precisely and formally set out, it is usually easy to recognize such a vision.

Visions need visionaries. Whether it is a prophet, like Zechariah, or someone known for special connections to the community, like John in Revelation, there is usually a credible human being to carry the vision. Very often (and here Daniel is an especially good example), there are stories or other materials that provide the credentials for the visionary. These credentials affirm the whole idea of a vision coming to Daniel or John or Zechariah or Isaiah. The fact that these seers have special relationships with God also provides a rationale for their being chosen vehicles for expressing visions, sometimes with the help of a heavenly interpreter, and then to clarify that vision for us.

WHY? ROLES AND FUNCTIONS

The visions described and interpreted by Daniel and John are intended for an elect group that has a special relationship with God. The visions are supposed to be difficult, impossible to understand without special knowledge given only to the small in-group. The subjects of oppression, conflict between good and evil, and the end of time all point rather clearly to particular settings and intentions for the visionary voice in the Bible. It is usually assumed that the folks who speak of these things are experiencing them, hoping at some point in the future for God to come and overturn the world as they know it, finally bringing salvation for the good guys and damnation for the bad ones. Some interpreters see this kind of vision as just a pipe dream, a vain hope for some reward at the end of time since there is precious little chance of such a reward in this world. Others, however, look at the practical effects of such a vision, things like the coalescing of community resolve and identity in the face of hardship, the increase in motivation to do good works now so that we can experience the rewards that come to those who suffer now but will ultimately be saved. All of this seems good. Thus, when things get bad, and seem to be getting worse, this simply indicates the time of deliverance is very close. We should therefore keep up our resolve and do the right things, being prepared for the day of the Lord that will come like a thief in the night, and very soon.

Viewed in this way, the visionary voice of scripture brings confidence to the elect, to the ones who understand the weird visions of Daniel or John, visions not intended for everyone. These visions bring comfort, reaffirming that we are right and the others are wrong. God will come to make all of this clear, delivering us from all the trials and tribulations of this present world. God is on our side, the visions seem to say!

These visions are ready and willing to assign guilt to the other. We know who is right and who is on God's side, and who is not. The oppressors are to be damned forever. These are not only the foreign powers that presently hold domination over the people. They are also members of our own community who have sided with the foreign powers, who have become impure by association with them, and who have betrayed God by their lack of faithfulness to the covenant. The intention of these visions, then, is to comfort a pretty small group of believers, ones who have not sold out.

The visionary voice puts things into a new and larger perspective. Things don't look good right now for the faithful. But the cosmic, heavenly perspectives given to Daniel and John and many others through visions make it clear that we are actually in pretty good shape. God is coming, and soon, to redress our problems and to put things into a new order. That new order will be so dramatically different that it requires us to think of new heavens and a new earth. Continuity with what we have experienced to this time is not possible.

In this sense the voice of the visionary is anti-establishment, very different from that of the historian. It is hard to imagine that the present institutions of this world, whether belonging to foreign powers or the people of God, will be the vehicles for God's radical transformation of the world and the final judgment. The visionary voice is not necessarily a cooperative voice, as there is a great deal of conflict inside and outside the community.

WHERE? THE SIGNIFICANCE OF PLACE

In order to understand where the visionary voice occurs most naturally and frequently in the Bible, we need to rehearse again the context that often produces, or at least makes possible, such visions and voices. Oppression and conflict are a big part of such context. Whether the group addressed by these visions is actually a minority or not, it usually believes it is—surrounded by enemies inside and outside the community of faith. Given such a social context, the scriptures that include such visions are grounded in the firm belief that things were not and are not intended to be like this. There is a disparity between life as it is and the promises for the people of God. Yes, the history of Israel is a history filled with sin and disobedience, judgment and punishment. But for a long time the chosen have been faithful in the face of foreign oppression, though many Israelites continue in their sinful ways. Torah's promises, continued into the Former Prophets, of a land filled with milk and honey are still valid.

Out of such a context come radical new visions of the end, an in-breaking of God's reign, putting an end to oppression and the disparity between scriptural promises and the reality in which we presently live. To see these promises as a future reality forces the visionary to speak of a radical disjunction between time as we know it now and that time when all will be well. Yes, Torah and Prophets and Gospels must and will be taken seriously, but revisionist history no longer fits in the world of our present experience.

In the Hebrew Bible we begin to see radical visions like this in parts of Isaiah, Joel, and Zechariah, but most of the prophetic voice still holds out for the promises of Torah to be fulfilled in time and space as we presently experience them. It is appropriate and understandable, then, that Daniel (a seer of visions quite different from most prophets) is found in the Writings, where the tensions between the already (Torah) and the not yet (Prophets) are found. It is in such a context of conversation about the new Israel that visions like those of Daniel live.

In the New Testament there is indeed something new, a new Torah, if you will, in the Gospels. But all of the New

Testament occurs in times like those of Daniel. There is no new promised land of milk and honey, just more and different oppressors. Therefore, as many have pointed out, not just Revelation, but virtually all of the New Testament is touched and colored by visionary voices. The visions of John may be the fullest and most dramatic, but evidence of this kind of envisioning of the future is found throughout the New Testament. This is a good reason to see the whole New Testament as a part of the Writings. The good news of Jesus must still be put into dialogue with the scriptural promise of earlier times. And, given the same disparities between promises of salvation in the past and our present experience, the voice of the visionary becomes a very real conversation partner for contemporary faithful living.

SO WHAT? SHAPING CONVERSATION

What does talking with the Bible as visionary today look like? It must first acknowledge that things have not changed much. We are still in situations where promises of old and present realities clash; where, on the one hand, hopes for a revitalized and reenergized community of faith grow dim for many, but where some believe God can and will fulfill promises for a good life, on the other. Yet, to imagine such fulfillment is getting more and more difficult. The times are getting worse, not better, and soon there must be some resolution to all of our suffering and oppression inside and outside our communities of faith.

Conversation with the visions found in Daniel and Revelation requires us to be open to a radical rethinking of how God will bring about our salvation. At the same time, the visionary voice reminds us that we are chosen, special, righteous, that we are doing what God needs and wants to be done in this world. Admittedly, there is often not a lot of corroboration for these beliefs in our church and world.

Indeed, within our own communities of faith there are those
who accuse us of having crazy dreams, asking for things
that are not possible, that God doesn't even want. And yet,
some remain convinced that a faithful vision includes commitments to particular places for education, to particular
mission priorities and strategies, to particular stances toward
non-believers, and to particular loyalties to our communities
of faith. We affirm these commitments even if they entail conflict with other institutions in our society. In short, there are
some places (not always the same place for everyone) in our
faith communities where we believe that God is in control,
despite all appearances to the contrary.

   All of the above are indications that we might be ready
to take the visionary voices of the Bible seriously. Time is
short. We must be faithful to God now, knowing that the end
is near. To converse with this voice is to take seriously the
immediacy of the vision and the call for faithful obedience
now, not later. Our ethical stance and response to folks in
need is grounded in the rhetoric of the visions that God will
come when we least expect, like a thief in the night. There is
no time to wait! We must expect and be ready for conflict.
Not everyone in our community of faith will agree with us,
but we will continue to live out the Gospel and Torah promises as best we can, knowing we will soon be with God. If
this sounds a bit scary, it is! And it raises the question we
must finally address . . . the question of how we can be in
conversation with and faithful to all the voices of scripture at
one and the same time.

STUDY QUESTIONS

Pick a favorite biblical text (or maybe two, one Old Testament and one New Testament) representative of the visionary, and briefly describe this voice by providing some answers to the following questions[1]:

- *What? Recognizing the Voice (Content and Form).* What does the voice of the visionary that you have chosen look like?
- *Why? Roles and Functions (Intention).* What is the agenda of the visionary in this text? Why is this story written and passed down to us?
- *Where? The Significance of Place (Setting and Canonical View).* In what particular part of scripture is this text found? How does this placement add to its meaning?
- *So What? Shaping Conversation (Application of Agenda; Formation).* Think of a situation in which this particular biblical voice might be especially valuable. What does a good conversation with this voice for the situation you have chosen look like? What positive things might this voice suggest? What new things might the voice suggest? Things you weren't necessarily looking for or maybe don't even want, but this voice wants factored in. . . .

---

1. For a fuller set of questions on these subjects, see the Introduction (pp. x–xii).

TALKING WITH THE BIBLE AS SAGE

PROVERBS 2:1–8

My child, if you accept my words
    and treasure up my commandments within you,
making your ear attentive to wisdom
    and inclining your heart to understanding;
if you indeed cry out for insight,
    and raise your voice for understanding;
if you seek it like silver,
    and search for it as for hidden treasures—
then you will understand the fear of the LORD
    and find the knowledge of God.
For the LORD gives wisdom;
    from his mouth come knowledge and understanding;
he stores up sound wisdom for the upright;
    he is a shield to those who walk blamelessly,
guarding the paths of justice
    and preserving the way of his faithful ones.

JOB 28:12–15, 23–28

But where shall wisdom be found?
    And where is the place of understanding?
Mortals do not know the way to it,
    and it is not found in the land of the living.

The deep says, "It is not in me,"
  and the sea says, "It is not with me."
It cannot be gotten for gold,
  and silver cannot be weighed out as its price. . . .
God understands the way to it,
  and he knows its place.
For he looks to the ends of the earth,
  and sees everything under the heavens.
When he gave to the wind its weight,
  and apportioned out the waters by measure;
when he made a decree for the rain,
  and a way for the thunderbolt;
then he saw it and declared it;
  he established it, and searched it out.
And he said to humankind,
"Truly, the fear of the Lord, that is wisdom;
  and to depart from evil is understanding."

MARK 4:1–9

Again he began to teach beside the sea. Such a very large crowd gathered around him that he got into a boat on the sea and sat there, while the whole crowd was beside the sea on the land. He began to teach them many things in parables, and in his teaching he said to them: "Listen! A sower went out to sow. And as he sowed, some seed fell on the path, and the birds came and ate it up. Other seed fell on rocky ground, where it did not have much soil, and it sprang up quickly, since it had no depth of soil. And when the sun rose, it was scorched; and since it had no root, it withered away. Other seed fell among thorns, and the thorns grew up and choked it, and it yielded no grain. Other seed fell into good soil and brought forth grain, growing up and increasing and yielding thirty and sixty and a hundredfold." And he said, "Let anyone with ears to hear listen!"

WHAT? RECOGNIZING THE VOICE

The sage has a significant presence in the Bible. While the influence of the sage is virtually everywhere, there are only a few books attributed to this group of writers, teachers, transmitters, preservers, and interpreters. Despite this, it is relatively easy to recognize this voice and to understand its roles and functions. Like the prophet, much of the wisdom literature of the sages is poetic in form. As we shall see, the particular character of Hebrew poetry, a parallelism that plays one topic off against another or uses the second half of the verse structure to develop the subject more fully, reflects an important part of the agenda of the sage.

Though the voice of the sage discusses all kinds of subjects, there are some that seem to be favorites. Nature and creation are frequent topics of study and reflection for the wise. Human experience is frequently discussed by the sage, especially the behavior of the good and the wicked. Often the sage is exploring questions of why we act the way we do and what the consequences of our actions will be.

While none of these topics seems particularly distinctive, it is important to note what is absent in these discussions of behavior, nature, and experience. There is rarely, if ever, a reference to Israel. There is rarely, if ever, a reference to the particular history of a person, a family, or a nation. Finally, and perhaps most striking, there is rarely, if ever, a reference to God as an actor in the world. All of this is most noticeable when compared to other biblical voices we have encountered. The voice of the sage, then, while embedded in many parts of scripture, is not steeped in the particular history and theology of Israel. At the same time, this voice is of utmost importance for scripture.

The vocabulary of the sage is distinctive. The language lifts up many behavioral characteristics and judgments: good and bad, wise and stupid, right and wrong. The basic definition of wisdom is often a topic of discussion, with the sage reflecting on experience to enlighten us. The sage frequently uses the rhetoric of a teacher or a learner. Clearly, with so many values and behavioral polarities, the voice of the sage is most often judgmental, making clear statements about what is right, what is wrong, what is good and wise, what is wrong and evil or stupid or ill-considered.

The sages use distinctive literary forms. The basic form is the Hebrew *mashal,* or proverb. In Hebrew, the proverb is a short aphoristic sentence, almost always a careful reflection on experience. Two examples of this kind of literary form are:

A perverse person spreads strife,
  and a whisperer separates close friends. (Prov. 16:28)

A cheerful heart is a good medicine,
  but a downcast spirit dries up the bones. (Prov. 17:22)

Both of these proverbs present behavioral reflections. The first develops and intensifies the first half of the verse with a concrete example in the second half. The second proverb provides an antithetical parallel to the cheerful heart, namely a downcast spirit.

There are many other literary forms frequently associated with the sage. The "happy is _____" formula, found in Psalm 1 and elsewhere, is another way to reflect on experience. Though not identical to this form, the Beatitudes in Matthew ring some of the same bells while raising challenging questions about the traditional teaching of the wise. The so-called numerical formulae, which can be found in many places in the Bible, are usually attributed to the sage. A classic example is:

There are six things that the LORD hates,
  seven that are an abomination to him:
haughty eyes, a lying tongue,
  and hands that shed innocent blood,

a heart that devises wicked plans,
  feet that hurry to run to evil,
a lying witness who testifies falsely,
  and one who sows discord in a family. (Prov. 6:16–19)

A variation on this form is found in the book of Amos: "For three transgressions of Damascus [the same form is subsequently used to accuse and judge many other neighboring nations, ultimately followed by Judah and Israel], and for four, I will not revoke the punishment" (Amos 1:3). This clearly reflects the voice of the sage, whose influence has been found in many parts of the Old Testament.[1]

The parables of Jesus are a wonderful example of the sage's voice in the New Testament. The passage cited from Mark 4 lifts up the call from Jesus for his listeners to engage in reflection on human and natural phenomena. The chapter continues with some examples. The basic call of Jesus in verse 9—"Let anyone with ears to hear listen"—is a paradigmatic example of what the sages want all of us to do.

The sages also use longer poems to speak of wisdom, nature, creation, and all sorts of behavioral issues. Proverbs 2 and Job 28, cited above, are good examples. Usually there is a larger goal for the longer poems, such as providing an impetus for obedience and allegiance to wisdom (Proverbs 2), or highlighting a critical way to understand the definition of wisdom (Job 28).

WHY? ROLES AND FUNCTIONS

One helpful way of defining and describing biblical wisdom is "skillful living."[2] So the sage teaches how we are to live skill-

---

1. See Donn F. Morgan, *Wisdom in the Old Testament Traditions* (Atlanta: John Knox Press, 1981).

2. See, for example, R. B. Y. Scott, *The Way of Wisdom* (New York: Macmillan, 1971).

fully and well. Such a goal for wisdom has serious theological implications, suggesting that God wants us to live life happily and well. To do so requires the use of observation and reason. Gaining wisdom, however, is less an intellectual process of study than it is using common sense to see patterns in our behavior and life. The sage sees those patterns and articulates some general teachings that apply to many.

The work of the sage is fundamentally concerned with discerning order in the world. It begins with a fairly optimistic and conservative assumption, namely that there *is* such an order to be discovered, expressed, and lived. That order is intimately tied to creation, as we hear Dame Wisdom speaking in Proverbs 8: "When he established the heavens, I was there . . . when he marked out the foundations of the earth, then I was beside him, like a master worker" (vv. 27, 29-30). To speak of good and evil, right and wrong, and all the other polarities so much a part of wisdom rhetoric is to pay attention to the order of the world.

As reflected in Proverbs 2, the one who has allegiance to wisdom will succeed and do well. This chapter reflects another basic task of the sage: to articulate and illustrate the way of wisdom, and its antithetical counterpart, foolishness, in the world. There is a system, often called "Two Ways," constructed around these contrasting examples of wise and foolish behavior. This system, built upon a theological foundation, affirms that wisdom leads to good things (success, prosperity, status) and foolishness leads to bad things (sickness, strife, judgment).

The way of God in the world is reflected in these systems, which are in turn associated with monarchy, family, and other institutions that provide order and stability and all good things. This wisdom, this way of God, this order, is not associated with Israel's particular history nor with God's special attention to those people. Rather, it is universal, applicable to and achievable by all. It can and should be learned and applied to successful living by Israel, yet it doesn't belong solely to them, but to the whole created order. The sage is an educator, caring deeply about learning from all things, good and bad. The wisdom the sage discovers applies to all people, though context always makes a difference.

A good example of the voice of a sage in a non-wisdom setting can be found in Psalm 112. Following after Psalm 111, which extols the wonderful deeds of God, lifts up the covenant, and closes with an aphorism about the wisdom of God and the fear of the LORD, Psalm 112 goes on to speak of the rewards received by those who fear the LORD, rewards that are not couched in the rhetoric of salvation history. Rather one obtains these rewards by acting on behalf of the poor, in generous and non-self-serving ways. The rhetoric and teaching of this psalm are grounded in human experience rather than in revelation.

While revelation is an important concept for the sage, it is not the revelation of God coming down to Sinai and giving the law, saying "do it and all will be well." Rather, revelation for the sage has more to do with the uncovering of something hidden or deeply interrelated with other things in the created order. So the sage is revealing a part of God's will and intention for the world by uncovering its order and the implications for how we are to live skillfully and well.

WHERE? THE SIGNIFICANCE OF PLACE

There is much evidence for the voice of the sage throughout the Bible. Torah and Prophets contain vocabulary and literary forms, which find their origins in wisdom literature, the primary place where the thought and writings of the sages are found. Whether or not these places actually reflect the influence of a tradition with a firm and clear institutional presence in ancient Israelite society is much debated.[3] What

---

3. See Morgan, *Wisdom in the Old Testament Traditions*.

is not debatable, however, is the fact that the sage's rhetoric, forms, and ways of thinking are found in Torah and Prophets. Regardless of how this happened, the voice of the sage is now present throughout the Bible. Given the universal appeal of the sage, this is not surprising. The thinking of the sage touched everyone in ancient Israel, and this is reflected in the two major divisions of Hebrew scripture, Torah and Prophets. Many New Testament scholars have also noted the importance of seeing Jesus as sage and teacher in the Gospels.

Nevertheless, the Writings are the place where the voice of the sage is most clear in the Hebrew Bible. There are many psalms that contain wisdom literary forms and thought. The wisdom literature of the Hebrew Bible—Proverbs, Job, Ecclesiastes—are also contained in the Writings. In this particular scriptural division, wisdom becomes a way of living and thinking that can be seen as a response to communities living with Torah and Prophets. So, for example, in the Writings we find a debate over who is a part of Israel and who is not (see, for example, the books of Ezra and Nehemiah). Also under consideration is Israel's relationship with the other nations of the world and the stories that are incorporated into worship rites that highlight or minimize those commonalities. In the midst of these communal identity questions, the sage asks Israel to contemplate wisdom and ways of living with each other that are not necessarily learned from revelation at Mount Sinai, but rather through careful observation of nature and the created order shared with all people.

The thinking of the sages in the Writings reveals much diversity. Sometimes, for example, the order in creation described by the sage is not clear or meaningful. Surely the books of Job and Ecclesiastes reflect such assessments. Questions about whether God is actually fair and consistent in dealing with human behavior, whether there really is a system of reward and punishment that works in a just way—these are some of the questions where difference of opinion occurs.

Even in the New Testament, where the proclamation of the salvation wrought for all by Jesus is front and center, there are debates over how all of this fits with the world's wisdom, whether or not this adequately explains the world for us, along with other questions often associated with the work and thought of the sages.[4] The voice of the sage is centered in the Bible as a response to how we must live in a world shaped and formed by Torah and Prophets and Jesus. It permeates all of scripture, providing a perspective for thought and reason that cannot and must not be dismissed.

SO WHAT? SHAPING CONVERSATION

Unlike some of the other voices encountered in the Bible, the voice of the sage is very clear about what it wants. The rhetoric of admonition, of exhortation, calling us to think about our world and especially the way we relate to one another, is very explicit. We are to study, to observe, to draw conclusions and to shape them into theories; we are to build theological systems that explain human behavior in terms of reward and punishment, good and bad, wise and foolish. We are to test these systems out, assessing them, being open to adjustments and revisions.

All of this work is done, however, on the assumption that there is a system that adequately explains human behavior, the knowledge of which will allow us to live well in the created

---

4. Both Ben Witherington, *Jesus the Sage: The Pilgrimage of Wisdom* (Minneapolis: Fortress Press, 1994) and Marcus J. Borg, *Meeting Jesus Again for the First Time: The Historical Jesus and the Heart of Contemporary Faith* (San Francisco: Harper, 1994), to cite but two examples, speak of Jesus as sage and wisdom teacher, referring to the wisdom forms associated with his teaching and the challenges he sometimes made to the establishment. The references Paul makes to the wisdom of this world, versus the knowledge gained through faith in Jesus Christ (see 1 Corinthians 1:18–2:5) are but one more instance of this dialogue between wisdom and more traditional revelatory tradition occurring in both the Hebrew Bible and the New Testament.

order. Acknowledging that God is responsible for such a system is key for the sage. Furthermore, as we have seen, the leaders of some central institutions in our society are players in these systems, proclaimers of values that we affirm. For example, the king is the head of the state, the priest has a special place in the cult, the father is the head of the family. The establishment and status quo orientation often associated with these institutions will not always seem true and compelling to modern ears. Neither did it for biblical ears! So the books of Job and Ecclesiastes debate the findings of their contemporary sage colleagues, and the life, death, and resurrection of Jesus turn the thinking of the wise and established folks upside down!

What will our conversation with the sage look like today? How can we affirm universal truths found in human behavior, and still be open to the new which might undermine the theories on which this keen observation rests? The quest for wisdom goes on!

STUDY QUESTIONS

Pick a favorite biblical text (or maybe two, one Old Testament and one New Testament) representative of the sage, and briefly describe this voice by providing some answers to the following questions[5]:

- *What? Recognizing the Voice (Content and Form).* What does the voice of the sage that you have chosen look like?
- *Why? Roles and Functions (Intention).* What is the agenda of the sage in this text? Why is this text written and passed down to us?

---

5. For a fuller set of questions on these subjects, see the Introduction (pp. x–xii).

- *Where? The Significance of Place (Setting and Canonical View).* In what particular part of scripture is this story found? How does this placement add to its meaning?
- *So What? Shaping Conversation (Application of Agenda; Formation).* Think of a situation in which this particular biblical voice might be especially valuable. What does a good conversation with this voice for the situation you have chosen look like? What positive things might this voice suggest? What new things might the voice suggest? Things you weren't necessarily looking for or maybe don't even want, but this voice wants factored in. . . .

10

TALKING WITH THE BIBLE AS LAMENTER AND SKEPTIC

PSALM 22:1–2

My God, my God, why have you forsaken me?

Why are you so far from helping me, from the words of my
  groaning?

O my God, I cry by day, but you do not answer;
  and by night, but find no rest.

PSALM 69:1–8

Save me, O God,
  for the waters have come up to my neck.

I sink in deep mire,
  where there is no foothold;

I have come into deep waters,
  and the flood sweeps over me.

I am weary with my crying;
  my throat is parched.

My eyes grow dim
  with waiting for my God.

More in number than the hairs of my head
  are those who hate me without cause;

many are those who would destroy me,
  my enemies who accuse me falsely.

What I did not steal
    must I now restore?
O God, you know my folly;
    the wrongs I have done are not hidden from you.
Do not let those who hope in you be put to shame
    because of me,
        O Lord God of hosts;
do not let those who seek you be dishonored because
    of me,
        O God of Israel.
It is for your sake that I have borne reproach,
    that shame has covered my face.
I have become a stranger to my kindred,
    an alien to my mother's children.

ECCLESIASTES 1:2–9

Vanity of vanities, says the Teacher,
    vanity of vanities! All is vanity.
What do people gain from all the toil
    at which they toil under the sun?
A generation goes, and a generation comes,
    but the earth remains forever.
The sun rises and the sun goes down,
    and hurries to the place where it rises.
The wind blows to the south,
    and goes around to the north;
round and round goes the wind,
    and on its circuits the wind returns.
All streams run to the sea,
    but the sea is not full;
to the place where the streams flow,
    there they continue to flow.
All things are wearisome;
    more than one can express;

the eye is not satisfied with seeing,
  or the ear filled with hearing.
What has been is what will be,
  and what has been done is what will be done;
  there is nothing new under the sun.

ECCLESIASTES 8:16–17

When I applied my mind to know wisdom, and to see the business that is done on earth, how one's eyes see sleep neither day nor night, then I saw all the work of God, that no one can find out what is happening under the sun. However much they may toil in seeking, they will not find it out; even though those who are wise claim to know, they cannot find it out.

MATTHEW 27:45–50

From noon on, darkness came over the whole land until three in the afternoon. And about three o'clock Jesus cried with a loud voice, "Eli, Eli, lema sabachthani?" that is, "My God, my God, why have you forsaken me?" When some of the bystanders heard it, they said, "This man is calling for Elijah." At once one of them ran and got a sponge, filled it with sour wine, put it on a stick, and gave it to him to drink. But the others said, "Wait, let us see whether Elijah will come to save him." Then Jesus cried again with a loud voice and breathed his last.

1 CORINTHIANS 1:10–13

Now I appeal to you, brothers and sisters, by the name of our Lord Jesus Christ, that all of you be in agreement and that there be no divisions among you, but that you be united in the same mind and the same purpose. For it has been reported to me by Chloe's people that there are quarrels among you, my brothers and sisters. What I mean is that each of you says, "I belong to Paul," or "I belong to Apollos," or "I belong to Cephas," or "I belong to Christ." Has Christ been divided? Was Paul crucified for you? Or were you baptized in the name of Paul?

WHAT? RECOGNIZING THE VOICE

The voices we examine in this chapter, lamenter and skeptic, are a bit different from those we have studied to this point. First of all, technically they belong to voices we have already encountered. The lamenter is usually found with the singer and pray-er, while the skeptic is most regularly found as a part of the sage's voice. The fact that we set aside a chapter for these seemingly minor voices needs explanation.

The voices of lamenter and skeptic often make us uncomfortable. Sometimes they raise hard questions about God and the world we live in, questions we would rather not address. At other times they speak of issues we don't want aired publically, things better kept in the privacy of our own hearts. They speak candidly and forcefully, with emotion and careful reasoning. Sometimes they raise questions that can't be answered.

Almost half of the psalms make use of lament. All three of the wisdom books of the sages have plenty of skepticism and serious questioning of the ways of God. For that reason alone we need to pay attention to these voices. Precisely because these voices are so important in the Bible, because they are heard in worship and in many places of everyday life, we need to address them separately. Yes, they belong to the voices of singers and pray-ers and sages. We need to remember and understand that their ultimate intentions push us in the direction of worship and praising God and to making sense of the world God has given us, learning how to live skillfully and well. But sometimes the hard questions of wisdom as found in Job or Ecclesiastes, and the cries of those who feel abandoned by God are distracting and disconcerting, especially when combined with songs of praise and affirmations of how wonderfully ordered the world is. Because of this, and because we dare not neglect or deny these voices, we place them, together, in a separate chapter. Our next chapter, which deals with some of the theological issues raised by the diversity of voices found in the Bible, is one place where we must attend to the constructive task of putting lament and praise, skeptical and affirmative views of the world together again.

The biblical voices we examine in this chapter are most often expressed poetically. It is fair to say that both of these voices begin with a problem, or sometimes many problems! So the psalmists, Jeremiah, David, and others recall the fall of the state, crimes of all sorts, disasters of every variety (famine, flood, storms), persecution inside and outside the community of faith, illness. Sometimes these problems are of an intensely personal nature, the kind we might hear in a confessional: abandonment by close friends, family problems, and the like.

But it isn't the topic that makes these voices distinctive, it is the fact that they are complaining to God! God is not only the recipient of lament, but also the object of complaint and accusation. Sometimes there is an acknowledgment of some personal or communal culpability for wrongdoing. Most often, however, there is not. Things are not good, and the folks complaining about this accept no responsibility for it. Whose fault is it that there is injustice in the world? Whose fault is it that there is poverty and crime and disappointment and disease and war and so many varieties of evil we hardly know how to begin describing them? For the psalmist, and for other biblical voices, the fault is God's! The system of reward and punishment, of receiving good things (milk and honey and all that), seems fundamentally a sound one in theory, but in practice God has neglected the people, and things are now out of control. So the psalmist cries out: "Why have you forsaken me? Why are you so far from helping me, from the words of my groaning?" (22:1). The lamenter, then, is not simply or primarily complaining that the world is filled with hardship and suffering, but rather there was a promise it would be otherwise, that a relationship with God would be filled with fair skies and smooth sailing. Alas, this is not the case, so this voice forcefully tells God to fix it!

Now the psalmists might have approached the problem in another way, namely to ask: "What went wrong?" When this question is asked by the sages and many lawgivers in the cult, the answer is, more often than not, "we did something wrong." We sinned. We ignored God's commands. We succumbed to temptation and greed, and we're only getting what we deserve. This affirmation of the retributional punishment-and-reward system often occurs even when the sin and the obvious fault are not clear. We just assume we must have done something wrong. It is precisely here that the voice of the skeptic or radical questioner may come in, questioning whether or not it's really our fault. The possibility that maybe we just don't understand how the system works, that bad things do happen to good people, and that much of the time we will be unable to explain why, are rejected. The book of Job is a good example of this. One way to look at this book is to see it as a radical questioning of the "two ways theology" (good behavior brings good living, and vice versa—see Psalm 1) of the sages. In effect, the sages are critiquing the sages! The system simply cannot explain the way the world is, nor, in any way we wish to accept, the way that God works in the world. Such a position can lead quickly to skepticism.

There are many literary forms used by lamenter and skeptic to address the problems we have noted. Many of them rely on dialogue. The psalmists complain to God, desperately wanting God to answer. The sages talk with each other, hoping to gain insight about difficult and painful topics. As harsh and difficult to hear as some of the complaints in the Bible are, they are finally calling for conversation between God and the community of faith.

WHY? ROLES AND FUNCTIONS

The primary purpose of the lament voice in the Bible is to make a significant contribution to prayer and worship. The voice of lament seeks to get God's attention. It reminds God of promises concerning health and wholeness, success and prosperity, and all the good things coming out of the covenantal relationship between God and the people. God needs to turn things around. God doesn't actually appear to be around much of the time, and this needs to change as well. From time to time there will be confession and an acknowledgment that we humans have actually contributed to the not-very-satisfactory situation in which we find ourselves. But most of the time, until we get to Paul and the New Testament at least, there isn't that much confession associated with lament. The lamenter wants to give the things that aren't going well back to God, to say in essence, this is your problem, not mine. Take it and fix it, as you promised!

Finally, as with most all the psalmists, the voice of the lamenter wants to move to praise. The lamenter's fundamental understanding is that real praise cannot be offered without acknowledging the problematic ways of the world, the things that aren't working and need to be fixed, the costs we all have paid for living in a world unlike the one promised to us. Yes, the situations that cause lament are hopefully temporary, but they are real and need to be addressed through complaint in prayer. Some of the most classic lament psalms, such as Psalms 22 and 69, both of which figure in the New Testament passion narratives, end with songs of praise. But the psalmist first had to lament, with all that entails, to get there.

Some would say that the sages are trying to do the impossible, to answer the unanswerable. We want a system that explains everything, rewarding us when we are good and punishing us when we are bad. We want a just society where all have equal value and opportunity, where greed and injustice and all the other things that oppress and depress us are no more. Further, we want to believe that we have been given the ability to build such a society, to live in harmony with our neighbors, to treat the stranger with respect.

The voices of lament and skepticism express doubt, raising concern about the inequities in our world, about those who set up "two ways" systems of reward and punishment, good and bad, systems that never adequately explain reality. And if they can't and don't explain reality, why would we have confidence in a god associated with such a system? These voices call us to be honest, to look at the world after we take off our rose-colored glasses. They call us to confess our ignorance. Maybe we will have to settle for mystery, leaving the rest with God. Acknowledging that there are some things we can't and won't ever understand, and that these things have much to do with God, this is a part of a spiritual journey with and a central task for these voices. Perhaps we will move toward skepticism, wondering whether there really is anything called wisdom that is worthy of the name. Perhaps we will be depressed by the truth reflected in the saying, "There is nothing new under the sun." Wherever we are on this journey of asking impenetrable questions, we do all of this as a part of a community that doesn't run away from these circumstances and the questions they raise.

WHERE? THE SIGNIFICANCE OF PLACE

The issues raised for lamenters and skeptics in the Bible are firmly rooted in Torah and Gospels, Prophets and Epistles. The promises of God for order, new life, peaceful communion or coexistence with our neighbors, prosperity, health, wholeness, and blessings of every kind are found in this literature. Yes, there may be a few problems along the way. However, careful obedience to the covenant and allegiance to the One who has saved and sustained the people of God will assure that these promises continue to be fulfilled. The systems of reward and punishment based on values made clear in Torah and Gospels work. And when these systems don't seem to work for us, individually or communally, the voices of lamenter and skeptic are significant for all of us.

We have already seen that the roles of pray-er, singer, and sage are located primarily in the literature of the Writings. The sages have central concerns for experience, positing an order to the world within which skillful living can occur. Sometimes, as they pursue these goals, questions concerning particular human experiences arise that challenge their assumptions of order, or the intentions and character of the One in whom the sages invest that order. At least some of the sages are, finally, not satisfied with the stock answers to these questions and suggest other, more radical, responses. All of this is compatible with the Writings, the section of the Bible that tries to make sense of a community committed to Torah and Prophets in the midst of difficult times.

Likewise, the singers and pray-ers of ancient Israel seek ways to give thanks and praise to God whenever possible. In the midst of major catastrophes, such as the fall of Jerusalem and the kingdom of Judah, the book of Lamentations (and a few psalms) is the most appropriate response. Illness and other more easily anticipated forms of challenge and suffering can also provide an impediment to praise and thanksgiving. In all of these cases, lament plays a central role in Israel's worship, a way of bringing God into the middle of these events and concerns, coming to a point of resolution (or at least acknowledgment), and moving again toward praise and thanksgiving.

It is important to note that both of these roles, the skeptic and the lamenter, are first addressing their questions and concerns and requests to God. Yes, there are social issues involved. Indeed, these issues have often been the starting point for both sage and lamenter, the place that caused the lament or radical rethinking about wisdom's approach to life's problems. But it is the theological questions raised that are primary. So the lament is addressed to God, not to our fellow community members. And the radical thinking about how the world really works, or doesn't, is meant to address the theological foundations of our values and behavior.

SO WHAT? SHAPING CONVERSATION

To be formed by the roles of lamenter and skeptic in the Bible is to look at the traditions of our communities of faith with honesty, candidness, and sensitivity. Boldness and the willingness to attend to difficult theological questions are central to the lamenter and radical-thinking sage, and to those who would follow in their scriptural stead.

Yet asking hard questions and being open to the dissonance created by mixing promises of old with present circumstances are not enough. To talk with these voices means also being ready to consider the hard answers we may receive. For many who experience loss and catastrophe today, there is no silver lining, nothing that provides satisfaction and confidence in God's ability to fix things. The voice of the visionary, for example, often doesn't work for lamenters and skeptics—it seems too incongruent with legitimate expectations coming out of covenantal relationships with God or the "two ways" theology governing human behavior. Sometimes we must live with the thought that even if God exists, He or She or It is so transcendent as to make little or no difference in our lives. Or again, sometimes we must live with the reality that praise will not easily come to our lips, being blocked by our suffering and disenchantment.

At the same time, however, to be shaped in part by these voices is to do our lamenting and our radical questioning in the context of worship and the community of faith. It is also to face our laments and skepticism in the midst of trying to live well, knowing that the desire, and ultimately our ability for the task depends on the One who is creator and sustainer of all.

STUDY QUESTIONS

Pick a favorite biblical text (or maybe two, one Old Testament and one New Testament) representative of the lamenter and skeptic, and briefly describe this voice by providing some answers to the following questions[1]:

- *What? Recognizing the Voice* (*Content and Form*). What does the voice of the lamenter or skeptic you have chosen look like?

- *Why? Roles and Functions* (*Intention*). What is the agenda of the lamenter or skeptic in this text? Why is this text written and passed down to us?

- *Where? The Significance of Place* (*Setting and Canonical View*). In what particular part of scripture is this story found? How does this placement add to its meaning?

- *So What? Shaping Conversation* (*Application of Agenda; Formation*). Think of a situation in which this particular biblical voice might be especially valuable. What does a good conversation with this voice for the situation you have chosen look like? What positive things might this voice suggest? What new things might the voice suggest? Things you weren't necessarily looking for or maybe don't even want, but this voice wants factored in. . . .

---

1. For a fuller set of questions on these subjects, see the Introduction (pp. x–xii).

PART

III

Inviting and Teaching

11

THE BIBLE AS GOD-TALK

ISAIAH 2:1–4

The word that Isaiah son of Amoz saw concerning Judah
and Jerusalem.

In days to come
the mountain of the LORD's house

shall be established as the highest of the mountains,
and shall be raised above the hills;

all the nations shall stream to it.

Many peoples shall come and say,

"Come, let us go up to the mountain of the LORD,
to the house of the God of Jacob;

that he may teach us his ways
and that we may walk in his paths."

For out of Zion shall go forth instruction,
and the word of the LORD from Jerusalem.

He shall judge between the nations,
and shall arbitrate for many peoples;

they shall beat their swords into plowshares,
and their spears into pruning hooks;

nation shall not lift up sword against nation,
neither shall they learn war any more.

JOEL 3:9–12

Proclaim this among the nations:
Prepare war,
   stir up the warriors.
Let all the soldiers draw near,
   let them come up.
Beat your plowshares into swords,
   and your pruning hooks into spears;
   let the weakling say, "I am a warrior."
Come quickly,
   all you nations all around,
   gather yourselves there.
Bring down your warriors, O LORD.
Let the nations rouse themselves,
   and come up to the valley of Jehoshaphat;
for there I will sit to judge
   all the neighboring nations.

JOHN 15:12, 17

"This is my commandment, that you love one another as I have loved you. . . . I am giving you these commands so that you may love one another."

REVELATION 16:5–7

And I heard the angel of the waters say,
"You are just, O Holy One, who are and were,
   for you have judged these things;
because they shed the blood of saints and prophets,
   you have given them blood to drink.
It is what they deserve!"
And I heard the altar respond,
"Yes, O Lord God, the Almighty,
   your judgments are true and just!"

At the conclusion of an overview of many biblical voices—in the presence of so much difference, so much diversity in one book claimed as authoritative by all—there is surely cause for rejoicing. Such a book is a mandate for tolerance, for inclusiveness, and for acceptance, enriching all who call it scripture. The Bible is a witness to one God, made known through many different manifestations and epiphanies.

At the same time, the presence of so much *theological* difference can be a problem for Christians. Here is one place where diversity can create complications. The one thing Christians (at least, Episcopalians) find difficult to share with one another is our thoughts about God. If our God needs to be bellicose, beating plowshares into swords, we are not interested in hearing that someone else's God is a lover of peace, beating swords into plowshares. If our God is filled with love and asks us to do likewise, we are not interested in a God who seems to delight in judgment and subsequent destruction. If our God is deeply identified with the established community institutions and a promulgator of uniformity, we don't want to hear that someone else, with other scriptural mandates, sees God as the champion of strangers and foreigners and threats to the status quo. To say, therefore, that we have many images of God in the Bible is usually not to suggest a place of easy unity.

Can the diversity and difference present in all the God-talk of the biblical voices ultimately lead us to enrichment and learning from one another? Another way to explore this question is: What might it look like for us to have conversations with all of these God-talkers? It is one thing to acknowledge their presence and to note their differences. But what if we were to talk with *all* of them, to be open to all their perspectives, to be open to formation and shaping by all? This is the promise and the potential of talking with the Bible. Instead of avoiding the voices that we find problematic, what if we were in conversation with both Isaiah of peace and Joel of war? What effect might this have on our Christian faith and ministry in times of struggle and change?

WHAT? RECOGNIZING THE VOICE

Despite many books written about Old and New Testament theologies, there is really no systematic theology in scripture. Rather, we have a lot of seemingly eclectic "God-talk"—talking about God, sharing experiences in which God has been perceived to be active, where significant relationships with God, the people, and certain individuals are paramount. The writers of the Bible, then, are most interested in the "what" question, in talking about and with the One who is closely associated with the roles and voices of the Bible, some of which we have examined.

Thus, for example, God is experienced and described as:

- a character in a story who:

  1. creates everything and is responsible for all;
  2. promises prosperity and success for both individuals and peoples;
  3. cares deeply about particular peoples, like Israel and Judah;

- one who is due praise and thanksgiving—and complaint and doubt;
- one who gives direction, often through the agency of the law, as a result of the covenantal relationship between God and people;
- one who breaks into the life of the people, bringing new things, recollecting old things (covenant, Torah), threatening and promising the people;

- one who cares about community and about the institutions that sustain community (cult, monarchy, state, clan);
- one who will finally call us and the whole world to judgment, perhaps sooner rather than later, in cataclysmic ways;
- one who wants all to live well in the created order and has given us the ability to do so;
- one who acts in ways that confuse us, even scare us, and who can seem absent when we are most in need.

In the midst of all this God-talk, there are some fairly significant and recurring polarities between, for example:

- Jesus and God,
- Jews (Israel) and Gentiles (foreign),
- the particular and the universal,
- lament/complaint and praise/thanksgiving,
- immanent and transcendent experiences of God.

WHY? ROLES AND FUNCTIONS

The rationales behind the ways we experience God, behind the "what" testimonies found in the voices of the Bible, usually focus on continuing and strengthening the relationship between people and God that brought the scriptures into being. First and foremost, these rationales express our experiences of salvation. The biblical voices testify to a journey from landlessness to a promised land filled with milk and honey. It is a journey from the foreign and strange to a place of familiarity and comfort. It marks the transition from slavery and death to freedom and life. Surely all of this is reason to speak of God, to tell the story!

As we have seen, the experience of salvation automatically and dramatically raises the "so what" question. Why new life? Why liberty? Why a new land? Why a new identity? The answer is usually found first in the covenant, in the relationship created and shaped by the salvation experience itself, the covenant between God and the people, between God and the world. From this covenantal relationship with God come other calls for special behavior or declarations of special status and general being: holiness, sanctification, purity, election.

Sometimes the disparity between the people's behavior and covenantal expectations results in God-talk filled with judgment. Then the focus may be on sin, on falling short, on any number of behaviors that, intentionally or not, trump service to neighbor and God. The judgment that follows takes a variety of forms.

Closely associated with a judgment rationale is the multifold experience of blessing and curse found in the scriptures. Blessing and curse are promised and flow from the covenant relationship between Israel and God. We have seen that the voices of singer and pray-er, of lamenter, sage, and lawgiver often use a system of reward and punishment to anchor these two very different experiences of blessing and curse. Sometimes there are horrific judgments on the sins of the leaders or the whole people, while at other times there are manifestations of God's continuing care for and direction of the people in the new land. In either case, there is a powerful testimony to God's continuing relationship with the people and active presence in their life.

More often than not, God-talk of the Bible is attached to particular institutions. So, for example, while we may speak of Abraham, Isaac, and Jacob as individuals, the clan structures they lead are very much a part of the Bible's concern and focus too. Likewise David, Saul, and Jesus, among others, focus us on the monarchy and kingship of particular peoples. And when we speak of Paul or Peter or Moses, we are focusing on the cult, the church, and the institutional manifestations of the relationship between God and the people.

Finally, both Old and New Testaments link God with the foreigner, the stranger, suggesting that God is indeed a God of the whole world. We hear this message through the voices of sages, who have always pushed for this universalistic perspective, as well as significant prophetic voices like those found in Isaiah, suggesting that Cyrus, king of Persia, will function as a messiah to deliver the people, once again, from slavery and bondage. Or it is the voice of Paul, speaking of God's great care and concern for the Gentiles. . . .

WHERE? THE SIGNIFICANCE OF PLACE

With the notable exception of the book of Esther, there is explicit God-talk in all parts of scripture. And even in Esther there are themes related to being the people of God in a foreign and hostile land. Indeed, it is hard to suggest there is one special scriptural place where talking about God is most significant. It is, however, clear enough that in Torah and Gospels we have God-talk of a different order, for there we hear and experience the foundational elements of the relationship between God and the people: salvation associated with the patriarchs; the exodus; and the life, death, and resurrection of Jesus. Without these, there is no special relationship between God and the people.

In Prophets, Writings, and Epistles (including Revelation), the focus is on faith and practice. God-talk then focuses on what the people have done or are doing, successfully and unsuccessfully, to live into the full relationship promised in Torah and Gospels.

In the scriptural house or canon, there are voices that have pride of place. They are not necessarily more important, but there is a sequence. Prayer, for example, or a prophetic oracle judging the people, presupposes a "what" and probably a "why," which are most often located in Torah and Gospels. The shapers of canon, then, are trying to organize the God-talk on the basis of certain priorities and sequences.

SO WHAT? SHAPING CONVERSATION

We come again to our central question: How can conversation with *all* the voices of God-talk shape us? What difference does talking with the Bible make as we look at the diversity and difference found there? Remember: these voices are not "objective." They are not trying to provide us with many different options, though perhaps the ancient collectors and organizers of the canon were. No, the voices of the Bible set forth strong rationales for their particular, and often conflicting, points of view. On the other hand, one of the intentions of a canon is for us to hear everything and everyone, to pay attention to *all* of this God-talk. In doing so we will also be more sensitive to the options for relationship within the scriptures, more open to the many ways in which God is seen and experienced, more able to relate one voice to another, more willing to listen, to stay in the same room with those with whom we differ.

We will also be more prepared to deal with challenges both inside and outside the Bible. This is, at least in part, because talking with all the biblical voices affirms that we are not alone. More important, there may even be, gracefully, some things to learn from those conversations with the folks with whom we differ.

Maybe, just maybe, God becomes a bit bigger, clearer, and more mysterious at the same time as a result of such conversations. Maybe even a bit more real? This might be the promise of talking with the Bible.

STUDY QUESTIONS

- How do we deal with the different theologies (pictures of God) in the Bible and the apparent fact that the biblical witnesses, and we, experience God differently?
- If the Bible contains all this difference, why can't the church?
- What's the difference between talking with the Bible and its different notions of God, and talking with a stranger today with a similar notion?
- What kind of companion or dialogue partner is the Bible here?

12

THE BIBLE AS FAITHFUL CONVERSATION PARTNER

MICAH 6:6–8

"With what shall I come before the LORD, and bow myself
   before God on high?

Shall I come before him with burnt-offerings, with calves a
   year old?

Will the LORD be pleased with thousands of rams, with ten
   thousands of rivers of oil?

Shall I give my firstborn for my transgression, the fruit of
   my body for the sin of my soul?"

He has told you, O mortal, what is good; and what does
   the LORD require of you but to do justice, and to love
   kindness, and to walk humbly with your God?

JOHN 3:16

For God so loved the world that he gave his only Son, so
that everyone who believes in him may not perish but may
have eternal life.

1 CORINTHIANS 13:1–3, 13

If I speak in the tongues of mortals and of angels, but do not
have love, I am a noisy gong or a clanging cymbal. And if
I have prophetic powers, and understand all mysteries and

all knowledge, and if I have all faith, so as to remove mountains, but do not have love, I am nothing. If I give away all
my possessions, and if I hand over my body so that I may
boast, but do not have love, I gain nothing. . . . And now
faith, hope, and love abide, these three; and the greatest of
these is love.

After looking at several important biblical voices, it seems
appropriate to return to the texts we first examined. How
do these fit with the voices we have studied? What kind of
conversations might we have with them? One of these texts
is from the Gospels, indicating a special foundational place
in scripture. This proclamation of the gift of Jesus, together
with similar and parallel messages found in other gospels and
in Torah, is always among the first texts used by evangelists.
Though John tells the story in his own special way, this passage
best fits the voice of the storyteller. We need to be in conversation with texts like this, to learn of the rock upon which the
community's faith is built, and from which its mission and "so
what" in the world flow. The other two texts we considered,
from Micah and 1 Corinthians, are located in the Prophets,
intentionally exploring how to live faithfully in light of the
covenantal relationship created because of God's deliverance
of the people.

These voices point to fundamentals of Christian faith and
practice. John sets forth the reason why the church was created and a central piece of its message. Micah and Paul boldly
state that faithfulness to God will require commitment to
justice and loving-kindness to our fellow human beings. The
test of our being in conversation with these biblical voices is
clear enough. If there is a confession and witness that Jesus
does indeed represent a salvific gift of God to the world, and
if that acknowledgment is accompanied by acts of love and
justice to others, then we have heard these voices and taken
them seriously.

Of course, there are many different ways to love, to act justly, and to understand what the gift of God in Jesus means. Different communities of faith interpret these voices in radically different ways, developing widely divergent strategies of witness and evangelism. Just as important, these voices themselves change as a believer lives and converses with them over a number of years. Love of neighbor may always be a part of our mission and faith, but how we understand this imperative often changes with time.

It is hardly surprising that these three texts would be foundational to the community of faith. These are voices that take us quickly and directly to the heart of the institution and speak directly to the benefits of being a member of the faith community. While the ways in which we act upon such messages change from time to time, the implications of the conversation are not cryptic. Indeed, these texts cry out for conversation, inviting a new relationship or sustaining an old one.

CONVERSING WITH THE MANY VOICES OF SCRIPTURE[1]

The scriptural canon or building is filled with many voices singing different songs, sometimes creating great dissonance. What does it mean to live in such a building, desiring to be in conversation and relationship with *all* of the voices contained therein? Among other things, here are some observations:

- It is impossible to embrace all biblical difference at one and the same time, at least in terms of living and decision-making.
- Such a scripture calls us to be open to the new.

---

1. See Donn Morgan, *Fighting with the Bible* and the bibliography cited there for treatments of diversity and difference in the Bible.

- To live with all biblical voices is to live in tension.
- We can't be judgmental and so sure of the truth.
- With increased familiarity we will be less confused by the variety of voices, better able to recognize old biblical friends and enemies.
- We will never be able to be in relationship with just one voice again.
- Dealing with biblical diversity and difference is part of a longer journey with each other, with scripture, with God.

To talk with the Bible is to push against a notion of canon within a canon, a recognition that all of us have favorites, that none of us is capable of treating all texts with the same attention. A personal canon within a canon explains, for example, our tendency to use different parts of the Bible to justify our own positions. However, the implication of viewing the Bible as a choir of voices suggests we must be in dialogue and conversation with all of them. We do not have the luxury of dismissing one of them just because we don't like them. Rather, we have learned that the different voices of scripture may be likened to a multi-paned window, providing an invaluable and complex perspective for our faithful living in the world.

SHAPING THE VOICES OF SCRIPTURE

As our own experiences of initial conversations with the Bible testify, there is clearly no one norm for talking with the Bible. We have stressed that the place where particular voices are found within the scriptural canon can make a big difference for their import. Furthermore, placement of these voices is not random, but clearly related to the functions and roles associated with the major divisions. So, when we ask whether there is a logic for conversation with the Bible, the structure of the biblical canon is one factor to consider.

While there are surely many ways to organize and present the voices of the Bible, we have ordered them in this way:

- *Initial Voices:* These are textual voices lifted up and emphasized to us by particular communities of faith who want to introduce the teachings of scripture and the central parts of the church's teachings.
- *Foundational Voices:* These voices include the storytellers and singers and pray-ers, who lift up two critically important functions for the community of faith: testimony to the wonderful acts of God in times past, and worship.
- *Voices of Relationship in Community:* The foundational acts of God that create community, sustained by song and prayer, are followed by voices of lawgivers and prophets. These voices lift up those activities central to being the people of God: living in covenantal relationship and openness to direction and guidance.
- *Voices of Continuity and Community Building:* The voice of the historian in ancient Israel builds upon the storyteller's foundation, creating a history focused on its institutions, monarchy, and cult. One of these histories ends with the exile of the kingdom of Judah. Another, a revisionist historian, retells the earlier history, extending it well into the post-exilic period when Israel is rebuilt and reestablished. The visionary voice speaks of the future when God's will for the community is completed. Coming out of times of oppression and difficulty, the visionary voice necessarily speaks of a radical breaking in of God when the good will finally be rewarded and the bad given their just desserts.
- *Voices of Reason and Protest:* Here we learn of the sage and wisdom, with a concern to live well according to the systems of reward and punishment, good and bad, built into the created order by God. This voice, sharing many

presuppositions and experiential teaching from other sages in other cultures, is an all-important component of living successfully and skillfully. The final voices of lamenter and skeptic, while actually belonging to the larger entities of singer and pray-er and sage, are singled out because of their relatively strong messages in the Hebrew Bible. Though they are minority voices, they are critically important for their honest complaint to God and hard reasoning when there are areas of incongruence between our experiences and the voices of, for example, the historian or storyteller or lawgiver or sage.

There is surely a developmental scheme underlying the presentation and organization of the biblical voices presented here. I believe there is a logical sequence that goes from story to law, a sequence that has its necessary counterparts in singers and pray-ers, on the side of the storytellers, and prophets, who need the relationship described by the lawgiver on the other. The voices of historian and visionary are logically placed after there is a people with a story, or so we presuppose here. At one level, the voice of the sage is always around in ancient Israel and in New Testament times. Its place in the canon reflects the chronological reality that its literature was collected and made a part of the people's scripture at a relatively late date. The voices of lamenter and skeptic are also heard in the community of faith from the beginning. But there is some logic to presenting the more critical voices after the others have been presented.

Finally, in this book we have framed the conversations we have with scriptural voices in terms of the actions of the community of faith. We *enter* the community and the house of scripture for the first time, getting our bearings. *Listening and learning* to the biblical voices, being in conversation, is the epitome of the learning community and the heart of our conversation. This is where, when, and how scripture forms us.

Assuming this formation and this learning, the faithful Christian is now ready for the hard but wonderful work of being in dialogue with scripture and with fellow believers about the heart of their faith, God. *Inviting and teaching*, witnessing to others about the richness of the whole biblical house, becomes an activity for the mature Christian and the means by which we start the cycle of formation and learning all over again.

There are certainly many other ways to present the voices of the Bible. I have intentionally tried not to locate these voices historically, nor do I presuppose that the sequence I use to organize them is premised on a historical sequence or development. Our presentation is based on a system that highlights the functions these voices have for scripture, functions that engage us in conversation. Those conversations, from my perspective, are not dependent upon knowing the history and dates of composition relative to one another. It is more important, I believe, to understand the relationship between prophet and lawgiver, between storyteller and sage, between visionary and historian. It is these relationships, based not necessarily on any proven historical interaction but rather on the intertwining of functions central to the people of God, that create a possibility of scriptural conversation and formation, then and now.

OTHER VOICES IN THE BIBLE: IDENTITIES, DEFINITIONS, AND MIXTURES

There are surely other ways to define and describe the voices of the Bible. Here we have not even been consistent in our terminology, focusing sometimes on the role of the voice (prophet, sage), sometimes on an especially important activity (singing, praying, lamenting), sometimes on that which the voice produces (history, vision). Clearly there are many ways to describe these voices and what a good conversation with them might look like.

As readers of this book study the particular voices of the Bible, I encourage you to find and describe other voices. For example, is there a voice for the correspondent? Think of Paul, that great letter writer. Does the form of the letter represent a particular kind of voice that subsumes or overrides the prophetic function of the apostle? I chose to say no to this question, but others might argue differently, developing a new scriptural voice to engage in conversation. While I think most of the biblical literature can fit into the voice categories presented here, there are certainly other possibilities.

Even when all agree that, for example, the texts of much of the latter half of Torah belong to the voice of the lawgiver, there are important interpretations and distinctions to be made. The function and role of law in the Old Testament, in the New Testament, and in our contemporary churches and society are much debated. Surely how a particular community views and uses law will have a great effect on its conversations with this biblical voice. My only plea is that we try to find ways to listen and converse, even when it seems apparent our minds are already made up. Surprises and changes have happened before and will happen again.

One important point to note concerns the purity and homogeneity of biblical voices. They aren't! It is difficult, if not impossible, to find a voice in the Bible that is not borrowing forms, rhetoric, and content from other voices. Sometimes this is blatantly obvious. So, for example, the storytellers and historians of Torah and the Former Prophets insert songs and prayers (the Song of the Sea in Exodus 15, the Song of Deborah in Judges 5, the song of Hannah in 1 Samuel 2) into their work. Others insert wisdom forms (Jotham's fable in Judges 9) or particular vocabulary borrowed from other voices. Most of this is actually unintentional, reflective of the process of borrowing and learning that everyone engages in. It would be more surprising to see a "pure" voice that betrayed little or no interaction with other voices and the traditions associated with them.

IMPLICATIONS FOR THE FUTURE: NEXT STEPS

The mandate that follows from seeing the Bible as a series of voices is clear: *We are to talk with the Bible, all of it.* We are to do this on a regular basis. Otherwise the relationship we gain through conversation will be lost. We can do this in many ways. We can commit ourselves to reading all the Bible through one or another of the programs available. Or we can listen for the particular voices of the Bible when we hear lectionary passages read, or any other time the Bible is used in our communities of faith. We should be ready to hear and interact with several biblical voices as we address challenges in our own lives. To listen to one voice is good, but hearing two helps us stay honest, more open to the new. Indeed, this is one of my strongest recommendations: always try to hear at least two biblical voices when intentionally putting the Bible into conversation with a contemporary issue or challenge. It will allow the Bible to speak more effectively, removing some of the risk of hearing the text say just what you want it to say.

Finally, in talking with the Bible we must be open to surprise in our conversation. Recently a student said to me, "I've been listening to the Bible for a long time and it always seems to say the same thing, there's no dialogue going on here, at least on the text's part." I wonder. G. K. Chesterton once said:

> Now, there is a law written in the darkest of the Books of Life, and it is this: If you look at a thing nine hundred and ninety-nine times, you are perfectly safe; if you look at it for

the thousandth time, you are in frightful danger of seeing it
for the first time.[2]

The biblical voice is stable and steady. But it can and does
change. It does speak in different ways at different times. *Talking with the Bible* seeks to find appropriate ways to recognize
the many voices of scripture and to open ourselves to listening.
Real conversation comes out of and strengthens relationship.
We are shaped and formed through this. It may take a thou-
sand times to hear the Bible in new ways, but the conversation
enriches us each of those times.

---

2. G. K. Chesterton, "The Napoleon of Notting Hill," quoted in Colin Dexter, *The
Wench is Dead* (New York: St. Martin's Press, 1990), 132.